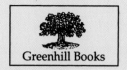

Greenhill Books

FIGHTERS
AT WAR

The story of air-to-air combat

Mike Spick

FIGHTERS
AT WAR

The story of air-to-air combat

Mike Spick

GREENHILL BOOKS, LONDON

Greenhill Books

Fighters At War
first published 1997 by Greenhill Books,
Lionel Leventhal Limited, Park House, 1 Russell Gardens,
London NW11 9NN

© Elephant Editions Limited, 1997

British Library Cataloguing in Publication Data
Spick, Mike
Fighters at war : the story of air-to-air combat
1. Fighter plane combat - History - 20th century
I. Title
623.7'464'0904

ISBN 1-85367-295-5

Credits

Editor: Ray Bonds
Design: Stephen Rowling
Photo research: Tony Moore
Typesetting and colour reproduction: SX Composing DTP
Printed and bound in Spain by Book Print, S.L.

Jacket and front matter photos:
Jacket front: France's small, lightweight Rafale scorches over the sand.
Jacket back:
Main pic: A US Navy F/A-18C Hornet climbs steeply above a desert mountain range.
Left: Cockpit of a WWI biplane fighter, gun ready for action.
Right: War-winning P-51Ds (and a P-51B at bottom of formation) from 8th Air Force's 361st FG in 1944.
Page 1: A USAF 18th TFW F-15C taking off with full afterburner.
Page 3: Tomahawks of RAF No. 26 Squadron practise over the English countryside in 1941.
Pages 4-5: A Bf 110C-4 of Luftwaffe ZG26 over the Western Desert in WWII.
Pages 6-7: An RAF Lightning warns a Soviet Tu-95 Bear bomber off its territory, a frequent Cold War activity.

The Author
Mike Spick is a leading commentator on military aviation, with nearly 40 books to his credit. His works, which include the internationally acclaimed *Designed for the Kill*, *Modern Air Combat* and *Luftwaffe Fighter Aces*, have been published in several languages. He maintains close ties with former and serving fighter pilots, and several distinguished test pilots, Americans and Russians among them. For many years a consultant to the Swiss-based helicopter program Project Atlas, he is currently a consultant to *AirForces Monthly* journal, and occasional contributor to *Air International*, *Air Enthusiast*, and the Malaysian-based *Asia Pacific Defense Review*.

Editor's acknowledgements
A great many people have provided valuable assistance in the preparation of this book, most notably by providing photographs, and the Editor extends his gratitude to all of them. A list of photo credits is given on page 144. Particular thanks are due to Bruce Robertson, who scoured his archive and loaned very many rare and interesting photographs, and to Jeremy Flack and Philip Jarrett who similarly gave up precious time in this way.

Contents

Introduction

A T THE GREAT international aerospace exhibitions, Le Bourget in France, and Farnborough in England, the stars are inevitably the fighters. As they thunder through the skies, performing often unbelievable gyrations, they are spectacular. But they are more than this; they represent the peak of national technology, the ultimate expression of national pride, and the first line of defense of national freedom. They carry detection systems of fantastic complexity and weapons of awesome capability. By comparison, macho machines such as fast cars, or automatic weapons pale into insignificance.

Whereas warfare is as old as the history of mankind, the fighter is very much of this century. It was born in

the stick-and-string era of the second decade, and honed in the crucible of battle during the First World War. Flying is an inherently dangerous occupation, although in peacetime in the modern era this is only when something goes wrong. But 85 years ago, flight was regarded as an activity only to be engaged in by consenting adults who were prepared to risk their lives.

In previous centuries, warfare was a two-dimensional combination of fire and movement, with the advantage going to the general who could out-maneuver his adversary. With the advent of the repeating rifle and the machine gun in the 20th Century the advantage passed to the defensive, and the Great War bogged down in the trenches. Movement was no more, and tens of thousands of lives were sacrificed to gain a few hundred yards. With the trenches stretching from the Swiss border to the North Sea, no outflanking moves were possible. Except one. The new-fangled flying machines could overfly the wire-strewn and bullet-swept front lines with ease.

Given that wars were won by surface forces, the most valuable roles for aircraft were reconnaisance and artillery spotting. This was closely followed by the dropping of primitve bombs, and machine-gunning enemy troops in the trenches. The fighter arose from the need to deny similar facilities to the enemy, and to protect friendly aircraft going about their routine tasks. At a later date this was called air superiority, and was defined as the ability to create favorable conditions for the conduct of surface operations, and the air operations which directly support them.

Manfred von Richthofen's famous red Dreidecker and the US Air Force's super-sophisticated F-16 are worlds apart in terms of technology, but one common denominator bridges the gap of generations: the skill of the pilot has always been a vital factor in air combat.

In practice, air superiority was both local and temporary, but the fighter pilots who gained it took on another aspect. The successful ones became heroes, not only defying the inherent dangers of flight, but assuming the mantle of the single-combat champions of times long gone. The world needed heroes; it also needed glamor. The first fighter pilots provided both, to become an inspiration to nations sickened of the apparently useless slaughter in the mud of the battlefields.

Even as the champions of old needed legendary weapons and enchanted armor to conquer, so the new knights of the air needed ever-improved machines in which to fight. Aircraft were designed to fill these needs; higher, faster, more powerful. Thus began the race for the best, culminating in the modern fighter and its weaponry. This is its story.

Mike Spick

Preface

NOON, LOCAL TIME, January 27 1991. Four F-15C Eagles of 53rd Tactical Fighter Squadron attached to the 4th Tactical Fighter Group, were patrolling at between 20,000 and 25,000ft (6,100-7,600m), about 40-60 miles (64-96km) north of the Kuwaiti border, due south of Baghdad. Their callsign was OPEC; while this was changed regularly, for this squadron it was always oil-associated. They were tasked with a defensive combat air patrol to protect the AWACS and some tankers.

About halfway through their six-hour patrol, AWACS asked them to move north, to an area south of Baghdad and just outside the SAM ring there. OPEC O1 and OPEC 02 had refueled

shortly before, but after about ten minutes on station the other two F-15s in the formation, OPEC 03 and 04, got low on fuel, and set off towards the tanker for a refill.

Shortly after, AWACS notified the two remaining Eagles, Captains Jay Denney in 84-0025 and Benjamin Powell in 84-0027, of possible hostiles (bogeys) westbound, about 100 miles (160km) east of their position and at about 3,000ft (900m). They immediately turned in that direction and began to search with their radars. Shortly after, they gained contact with the bogeys, which by now were about 60-70 miles (96-113km) due east of them and closing fast. The two F-15s heading for the tanker asked whether they should turn back to

Below: Controllers in a boeing E-3 Sentry like this asked OPEC Flight to move north, then warned them of bogeys westbound. From this a successful interception resulted.

help but, as it appeared that there were only two bogeys, Jay Denney, the flight leader, told them to carry on and refuel, while his element of two Eagles continued the intercept.

OPEC 01 and 02 soon confirmed that their contacts were hostile (bandits), and continued on a head-on interception course. As the range dwindled to about 35-40 miles (56-64km), the Iraqi aircraft, probably alerted to the presence of F-15s by their radar warning receivers, turned through 180 degrees and headed eastwards, directly away from the American fighters. This was fairly typical Iraqi behaviour; they usually turned and ran whenever Coalition fighters got to within 35 miles (56km) of them, making it difficult for them to be caught.

At this point, OPEC 01 and 02 broke radar lock and switched their radars to search mode. By doing so they hoped that the Iraqis' radar warning indicator would clear itself. With no apparent threat, they might just turn back.

By this time the Iraqi fighters were close to the Iranian border, which they had probably not been cleared to cross. At this point they changed course to north-west and flew parallel to the border. Denney and Powell selected an interception heading and went after them. Powell takes up the story:

"Until we got within 20 miles (32km) of them, we thought the formation had one or two planes in it. But then the formation split apart and we could distinguish three individual aircraft on our radar scopes. We closed on a beam intercept, rolled out into a tail chase at about 15 miles (24km) behind

the Iraqi aircraft. At that point we took our sort: prioritized the targets and assigned them to make sure we took separate guys. We took final locks and at this point the Iraqis descended from about 3,000ft (900m) down to 50ft (15m), still heading northwest, towards Baghdad.

"One of the things that puzzled us about their actions was that they continued to fly at a medium airspeed: 350kt (650km/hr) – we should never have been able to run them down from the back if they had sped up. We had our throttles as far forward as they would go, afterburners on, so we were doing something like Mach 1.2, say 800kt (1,480km/hr).

Above: Low on fuel, two Eagles of OPEC Flight were directed by the AWACS towards a tanker. It was at this moment that the bogeys were detected, but as it appeared that there were only two of them, the Eagles carried on to the tanker.

Left: Inside the Sentry a team of controllers continued to monitor the situation as the two remaining F-15Cs closed on the bogeys. Still there appeared to be only two hostile aircraft on the screen.

Below: As the bogeys neared the border with Iran they changed course. Contrails streamed from the wingtips as the Eagles reefed hard round onto an interception course.

"As we closed, my flight lead and I both took AIM-7 shots outside of visual range. Both of those missiles were misses. As we continued to close I picked up a tally on the aircraft: by eye I visually identified them as three MiG-23 Floggers. The lead was about five miles (8km) ahead of the tail, with the third one off to the left between them. My radar was locked on to the Flogger to the left, Jay was locked on to the plane in the rear.

"This whole time we'd been up at about 30,000ft (9,150m), simply because we knew we were in an area with heavy SAM and AAA defenses and we wanted to avoid ground fire. But at this point we both put the airplanes into steep dives, sinking down to around 6,000ft (1,800m). As I closed to within about 2½ miles (4km) of my contact I saw that the target was not in fact a single aircraft. He had a wingman: it was a Mirage F.1 flying in close fingertip formation. I closed on their stern, and as I was about to fire my second missile I saw Jay shoot an AIM-9 Sidewinder heat-seeking missile at his target. The missile made a straight beeline and blew up the Flogger: it just exploded in a fireball.

"Two seconds after that I fired my own missiles: radar-guided AIM-7 Sparrows. Both the F.1 Mirage and the Flogger were hit. The Flogger took a direct hit and just exploded in a fireball. The other missile detonated about 5-6ft (2m) off the Mirage's wingtip and that set off a secondary explosion. The plane just coasted into the ground and impacted five seconds later.

"Then I looked back towards the right, at the flight leader and the remaining Flogger, and I saw that the flight lead had closed to within 9,000ft (2,750m) of the MiG. He fired a second AIM-9, and that was also a direct hit. We saw this pilot eject and a parachute come out of the aircraft. There were no parachutes from the other aircraft.

"By now we were at low altitude in an area with a high concentration of enemy fire, so we egressed as quickly as possible – we ejected our fuel tanks to get rid of some drag on the aircraft, did essentially a vertical climb to get as high as possible, and then went back to our CAP".

The above account is fairly typical of air combat during the Gulf War, inasmuch as most Iraqi fighter pilots, undertrained and relatively ill-equipped, mainly sought to avoid their opponents. The Eagles were warned in good time by E-3 Sentry AWACS aircraft, and detected their opponents and positively identified them as hostile when well out of range.

An interesting point here is that OPEC Flight remained at high altitude until the final phase of the interception. While this was ostensibly to keep outside the ground defense envelope, it also gave a speed advantage to increase closure rate. By contrast, the Iraqis stayed low, presumably using their on-board radar in look-up mode. Level and look-up modes use pulse radar; look-down requires pulse-Doppler. As on any given piece of equipment the latter is rather shorter-ranged than pulse radar, the inference must be that the Iraqis hoped to arrive within radar range before the Americans could do so.

The ruse failed. Even in pulse-Doppler look-down mode, the radar of the F-15C was much longer ranged than the Russian kit carried by the Iraqi MiG-23s. OPEC Flight detected the bandits well back and their radars locked on before the Iraqis could even manage initial detection. Warned of a hostile radar lock long before they were in position to attack, and expecting

missiles to come whistling about their ears at any second, the Iraqi pilots sensibly put discretion before valor. They "legged it"!

Unfortunately for them, they were trapped against a hostile frontier, but with the radar lock apparently broken the threat seemed to have vanished. Flying at economical cruising speed, they followed the border north-westwards. But then their radar warning system once more told them that they were being targeted, and they hit the deck. Whether they saw the two Sparrow missiles flashing past them we cannot be certain, but it seems unlikely, as the Iraqi formation made no attempt to split up or accelerate away.

Why did the Sparrows fail? There are many possible reasons, quite apart from the quite obvious one of malfunction. Sparrow uses semi-

Above: A flight of F-15Cs as seen from the cockpit of a two-seater Eagle. The all-round view from the cockpit is superb; essential for an air superiority fighter in close combat.

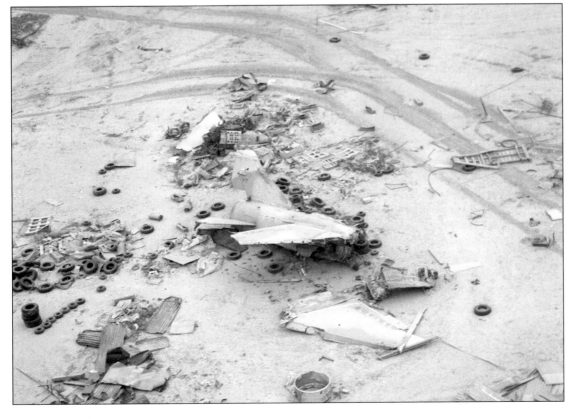

Left: The remains of an Iraqi MiG-23 after being shot down. A direct hit by a big missile like Sparrow is devastating. Even a near miss explosion is generally lethal.

active radar homing (SARH), in which the radar of the parent fighter illuminates the target, and the missile seeker homes on the reflected energy. A simple analogy is shining a torch at a target and aiming at the illuminated shape. In the look-down pulse-Doppler mode, background echoes from the surface have to be screened out, making the task of the missile much harder than if it had been launched against a target outlined against a clear sky. In other words, the torch shows up things other than the target, and the missile homes on the wrong one.

Then, while radar is excellent at providing range and relative speeds, angular discrimination is relatively poor. This does not help accuracy. Until the range closed to under 20 miles (32km), OPEC 01 and 02 thought they were dealing with just two aircraft; only at this point did their radars show three machines, while not until visual range was reached did they realize they had four to deal with. Radar could simply not pick out individual aircraft flying in very close formation. In any case, air-to-air missiles are not yet ten feet tall; no missile gives 100 per cent results.

Another point here is that SARH missiles work best against targets with a high speed differential, especially in the look-down shoot-down mode. Pulse-Doppler radar works by screening out returns moving in conformity with the flightpath; consequently it is more effective against a head-on high-closure rate target, than one in a tail-chase situation. The simple answer is that both Sparrows missed, probably through no fault of the shooters.

When the distance closed to knife range, it gave a choice of missiles. The heat-seeking Sidewinder works best against the hot tailpipe of a rear aspect target, and Jay Denney in OPEC 01 had no

hesitation in using it against two MiG-23s in quick succession. Both shots were successful.

By contrast, Powell launched two Sparrows against his targets, scoring a direct hit on the

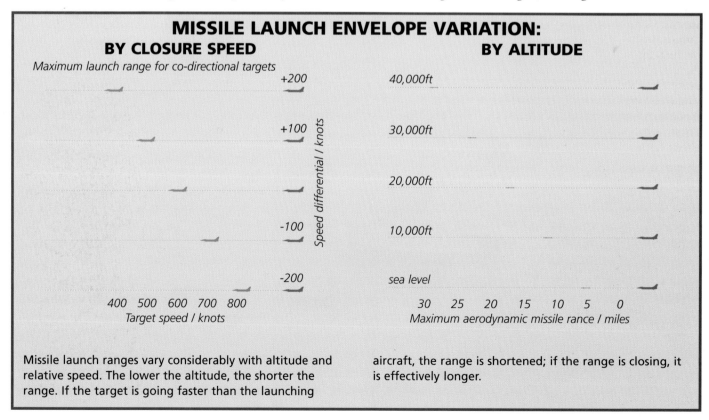

MISSILE LAUNCH ENVELOPE VARIATION:
BY CLOSURE SPEED
Maximum launch range for co-directional targets

+200

+100

Speed differential / knots

-100

-200

400 500 600 700 800
Target speed / knots

BY ALTITUDE

40,000ft

30,000ft

20,000ft

10,000ft

sea level

30   25   20   15   10   5   0
Maximum aerodynamic missile rance / miles

Missile launch ranges vary considerably with altitude and relative speed. The lower the altitude, the shorter the range. If the target is going faster than the launching aircraft, the range is shortened; if the range is closing, it is effectively longer.

MiG-23, and a miss near enough to be lethal on the accompanying Mirage F.1, which flew into the ground within five seconds.

This quadruple victory, scored within a matter of minutes, clearly demonstrated the advantages of superior technology, tactics, and training. Yet it was more than this. AWACS aircraft gave early warning of threat aircraft while they were still far beyond the range of fighter radar, while inflight refueling tankers enabled the Eagles to roam where they would and carry out six hour patrols, regardless of theoretical ranges on internal fuel and drop tanks. These force multipliers vastly increased the effectiveness of the fighters in all departments.

In addition, the air war was in its tenth day. The Iraqi early warning detection, command and control system lay in ruins. The situational awareness of the Iraqi fighter pilots was more or less confined to what they could see "out of the window", whereas the Coalition pilots had the full picture.

Three-quarters of a century earlier, fighting aircraft were sent on patrol in an attempt to dominate a brief patch of sky for an even briefer period. The contrast between the war they fought and the air combat over Iraq was almost infinite. The following pages fill in the gaps as to how this came about.

Above: An F-15C peels off. High speed at high altitude allows rapid overtaking, but often it is necessary to go down to attack.

Below: An F-15C Eagle takes off on a routine patrol from its Saudi Arabian base.

Cavalry of the Clouds
1914-1918

The Voisin LA was known as the 'chicken coop' by the French Air Service. In the hands of Josef Frantz and Louis Quénault the type scored the first air combat victory in history. Its main use was as a bomber in which role it is seen here in RNAS service.

EVEN BEFORE the outbreak of the Great War, the potential of the airplane for reconnaissance had been recognized. When in the late summer of 1914, German armies swept across Belgium and France, its value was proven. Air units began to take over the function of light cavalry, and when the German advance was finally halted, and the war ground to a halt in trench lines which stretched from the Swiss border to the coast of Flanders, there was no alternative. From being merely a useful supplement, air reconnaissance became almost the only means of finding out what the enemy was doing behind his own lines.

In previous centuries, a good light cavalry squadron prided itself not only on the quality of the intelligence that it gathered, but on denying similar facilities to the enemy. The old tradition applied equally to the new arm, and fighting in the air was the inevitable outcome. The problem was how? There was no precedent for combat between airplanes. The next year or so saw a great deal of trial and error; mainly the latter.

The first reconnaissance airplanes flew unarmed. If machines from opposing nations met in the air, they could only wave to each other and continue their respective missions. This state of affairs could not be allowed to continue. Observers started to carry rifles, carbines, and even pistols.

On October 15 1914, Louis Strange of 5 Squadron, Royal Flying Corps, intercepted a German Aviatik. After a lengthy pursuit, he finally closed the range, and his observer stood up, pointed his rifle over the top of the plane, and fired 70 shots. The similarly armed German observer fired back. So far as is known, no hits were scored, and the Aviatik escaped into cloud. Better weaponry was obviously badly needed.

Equipping the observer with a machine gun was the obvious answer, as the pilot was fully occupied in flying the airplane. But the drag and weight of the gun and its ammunition reduced performance of the early machines to the point where they had little chance of catching an opponent.

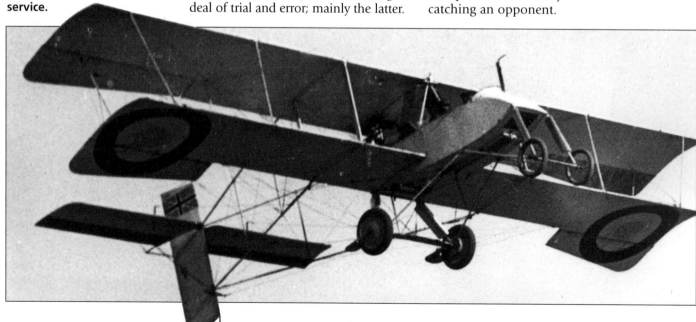

Even then, the best way of using the machine gun was unclear. Firing directly ahead was in those days a good way to shoot off one's own propeller, which was not the object of the exercise. Many participants visualized flying close alongside their opponents, exchanging naval-style broadsides. Virtually all the theories of the time assumed that an opponent would take no evasive action; a totally unwarranted assumption!

In fact, the way had been shown ten days before Strange's fruitless combat. High above the Belgian village of Jamoigne flew a French Voisin 3 reconnaissance biplane of Escadrille V 24. Of pusher configuration, it had a central nacelle holding two seats in tandem, behind which was a 120hp Salmson-Canton-Unné 9M water-cooled engine. The tail surfaces were carried on booms projecting from the wings. The maze of struts and wires which resulted caused the Voisin to become familiarly known as the "chicken coop".

It was slow, and its rate of climb was derisory. But with its propeller located behind the crewmen, it had an unobstructed field of fire forward for its Hotchkiss machine gun.

Suddenly a German Aviatik B.1 appeared below. The French pilot, Joseph Frantz, warned his observer, Louis Quénault, and launched his ungainly Voisin into a shallow dive, accelerating to close the range.

Quénault struggled upright against the slipstream; leaned forward and manned the gun. Balancing precariously, half out of the open cockpit, he aimed and fired.

Up to this moment, no airplane had ever been shot down by another airplane, and German pilot Wilhelm Schlichting may well

A product of the Royal Aircraft Factory, the two-seater FE.2b played a major role in countering the Fokker Scourge. Seen here is one of only two FE.2cs built as night-fighters. It was replaced from July 1916 by the more powerful FE.2d.

An Aviatik C.1a of the Luftstreitkräfte. The B.1 model shot down by Frantz and Quénault had the observer seated in front of the pilot, from where shooting back at an attacker was very difficult.

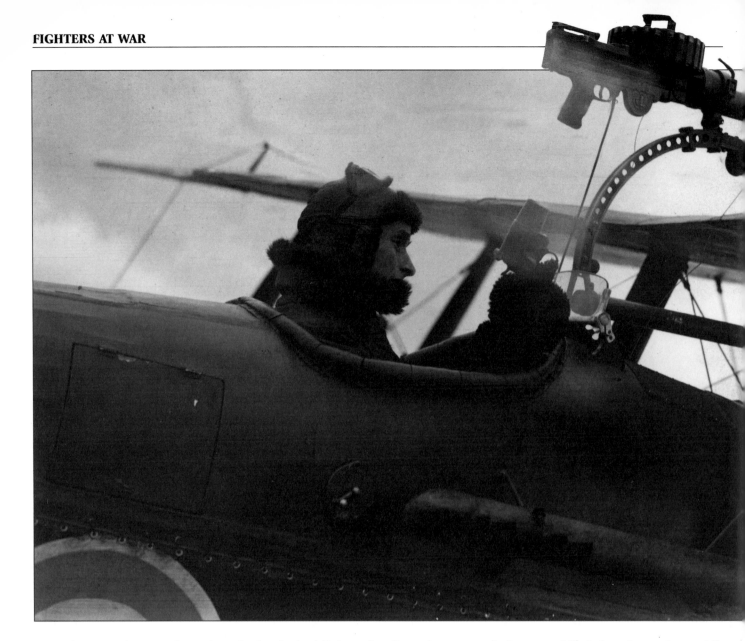

Mounting a Lewis gun above the top plane from where it could fire above the propeller disk was an early method of allowing an airplane to fire straight ahead. To change the ammunition drum, the gun was pulled down the curved slide. See also the Aldiss telescopic sight.

have thought that he had little to fear from the lumbering French biplane. A stream of bullets from the Hotchkiss suddenly awakened him to his peril, and he turned, both to avoid fire and to give his observer, Fritz von Zangen, a chance of shooting back. Frantz, using the speed of his dive, turned with him, keeping slightly low so that the Aviatik's tail masked the German observer's gun. Meanwhile Quénault poured in burst after burst at close range.

Finally the hard-used Hotchkiss jammed, but the damage had been done. Flames licked from the stricken Aviatik, and spread as it dived

towards the ground far below. It was the world's first air combat victory.

The victory of the Voisin was of course a fluke. It had been in exactly the right place at precisely the right time; something unlikely to recur often. What was really needed was an airplane with the performance to catch an enemy and force battle upon it, able to carry a machine gun, and to fire directly forward at a fleeing opponent.

The problems of accurately aiming a swivelling machine gun at an airplane from an airplane were particularly intractable. Deflection shooting is an art that few master. Add gravity

GUNNERY PROBLEMS

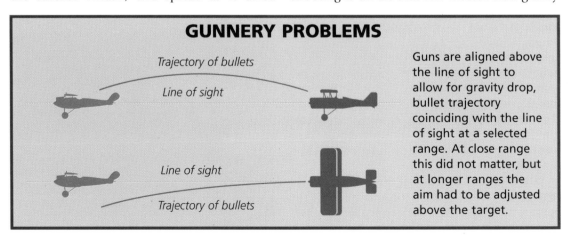

Guns are aligned above the line of sight to allow for gravity drop, bullet trajectory coinciding with the line of sight at a selected range. At close range this did not matter, but at longer ranges the aim had to be adjusted above the target.

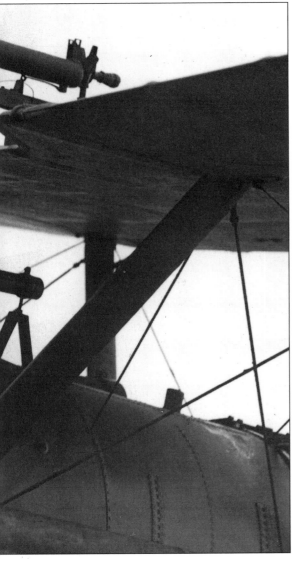

Ground gunnery was extensively practised on devices like this twin Lewis with a fixed ring and bead sight. However, air-to-air firing was far more complicated, especially when the airplane was maneuvring.

drop, then bullet trail and target precession, which are caused by relative motions of shooter and target, vibration due to a less than rigid mounting, and the buffeting of the slipstream, and it becomes difficult for even a marksman to hit anything except at extremely close range.

A fixed, forward-firing gun minimises many of these problems. The mounting can be much more rigid, while the firer does not have to struggle against the slipstream. Target precession is avoided altogether, while a firing position directly astern and in level flight eliminates deflection and bullet trail.

Therefore the future fighter had ideally to be a single-seater with at least one fixed, forward firing gun. This left two choices. The pusher airplane, with its "canary cage" of struts and wires carrying the tail surfaces, was aerodynamically inefficient, and power for power its use involved a significant performance penalty. The tractor airplane, with the engine and propeller at the front, was far better, if only the means could be found to allow a machine gun to be fired directly ahead.

Unable to resolve this problem, the RFC devised a scheme with carbines, then Lewis guns, lashed to the forward fuselage and canted outwards at an angle to miss the propeller disc. This scheme, which called for close formation flying at exactly the correct angle, was soon abandoned.

What was needed was a device to synchronize a machine gun with the propeller, so that it only fired when the blades were not in line with the muzzle. Even before the war, engineers had been working on the problem. Synchronization gear (often wrongly called interrupter gear), had been invented in France prewar, but its development was halted by hang-fire rounds – bullets which detonated slightly late due to manufacturing faults. To overcome this, Raymond Saulnier proposed fitting steel wedges to the propeller blades to deflect faulty ammunition. As each deflection would transmit a shock to the engine, the risks were judged to be unacceptable in peacetime.

Pioneer French aviator Roland Garros had joined the Aviation Militaire at the outbreak of war, and by the end of the year was flying with Escadrille MS 26. Knowing of Saulnier's work, he asked for the synchronization gear to be fitted to his airplane. With war raging, different standards applied. The problem with hangfire rounds remained, and finally the synchronization gear was discarded and only the wedges were fitted.

This Morane-Saulnier S used wing warping rather than ailerons and an all flying tail, which made it very sensitive in pitch. Very maneuvrable, and fast for its day, it was tricky to fly, and was built in only small numbers.

After some weeks, Garros rejoined his unit near Dunkirk. On April 1 1915, flying his Hotchkiss-armed and wedge-fitted Morane Parasol, he shot down an Albatros two-seater. More victories followed and Garros was widely acclaimed. Then on April 19 he was hit by ground fire and landed in German-held territory. He was taken prisoner, and his aircraft was closely examined by the Luftstreitkräfte.

The German Air Service had become concerned by Garros's widely publicized string of successes which, although humble in absolute terms, were outstanding at the time. This made them aware of the value of the fixed, forward-firing machine gun.

Advice was sought from the Dutch aircraft designer Antony Fokker. Engineers on his staff, aware of a synchronization gear patented during 1913 by Swiss engineer Franz Schneider, quickly adapted it for German use. The result was the Fokker Eindecker, the world's first true fighter airplane.

THE FIRST FIGHTERS

At first, there was little specialization. Only rarely did squadrons and sections fly the same airplane type, and all undertook the same missions. Some men showed a flair for certain tasks and to a degree were allowed to specialize. As RFC pilot Duncan Grinnell-Milne later wrote: "By a fortunate succession of accidents, my own role in the squadron (No 16) became gradually more that of a fighting pilot than of an artillery spotter or photographer." Old habits died hard; changes were generally forced by circumstances.

The first Eindeckers to arrive at the front were shared piecemeal among existing units. Flight Section 62, based at Douai, received two, and it

Max Immelmann, the Eagle of Lille, with the wreckage of his seventh victim, a Morane Parasol of No 3 Squadron RFC. He was killed on June 18 1916 when his Eindecker broke up during a fight with FE.2bs of 25 Sqn RFC.

FOKKER E.III EINDECKER

Dimensions: Span 31ft 2¾in (9.52m);
Length 23ft 7½in (7.2m); Height 7ft 10½in (2.4m);
Wing area 172.8sq.ft (16m²).
Power: One Oberursel U1 rotary engine rated at 100hp.
Weights: Empty 878lb (398kg); Loaded 1,342lb (609kg).
Performance: Maximum speed 87mph (140km/hr); Ceiling 11,500ft (3,505m); Climb 30 mins to 9,843ft (3,000m); Endurance 1½hr.
Armament: One fixed Spandau machine gun, belt fed with 500 rounds.
In service: 1915/1916.

The Eindecker was the first true fighter aircraft. By the standards of the day its performance was unexceptional, while the use of wing-warping for lateral control limited its agility. Its one tremendous advantage lay in its fixed gun which fired through the propeller disc, and was aimed by pointing the whole machine at the target. A monoplane, it was considered quite difficult to see at any distance compared to the biplanes of the era, and many of its victories were gained by exploiting tactical surprise. Although not built in any great numbers, it cut a deadly swathe through its British and French opponents in the latter half of 1915, but was outmatched by Allied fighters in the following year.

ALBATROS DV

Dimensions: Span 29ft 8in (9.05m);
Length 24ft ½in(7.33m); Height 8ft 10¼in (2.7m);
Wing area 229sq.ft (21.28m²).
Power: One Mercedes D.IIIa inline engine rated at 180hp.
Weights: Empty 1,511lb (687kg); Loaded 2,061lb (937kg).
Performance: Maximum speed 116mph (187km/hr);
Ceiling 18,700ft (5,700m); Climb 4 min to 3,280ft
(1,000m); Endurance 2hr.
Armament: Two belt-fed fixed Spandau machine guns.
In Service: 1917/1918.

The Albatros series of fighters first entered service in the autumn of 1916, in the sleek and shark-like shape of the D.1. With its new machine, the Luftstreitkräfte outfought the DH 2s and Nieuports then in Allied service. In early 1917 the D.1 and D.2 were supplanted by the superb D.III, of which Werner Voss and Richthofen were the leading exponents. When with the advent of newer Allied fighters later that year the D.III was outclassed, it

was replaced by the D.V. Although the series exhibited serious structural weaknesses, they were numerically the most important German fighters of the war.

was this section that led the way in finding the best means of using the new fighter.

It so happened that Section 62 contained two outstanding young pilots; Oswald Boelcke, who had already started to make a name for himself; and new boy Max Immelmann. These two were largely responsible for creating the Eindecker legend.

Immelmann, who flew almost exclusively against the British, became famous for the development of a maneuver that bears his name: the Immelmann Turn. Nowadays any attempt to define it precisely ends in a welter of controversy, but certainly it was a combat maneuver which used the vertical plane, allowing attacks to be made in quick succession.

THE IMMELMANN TURN

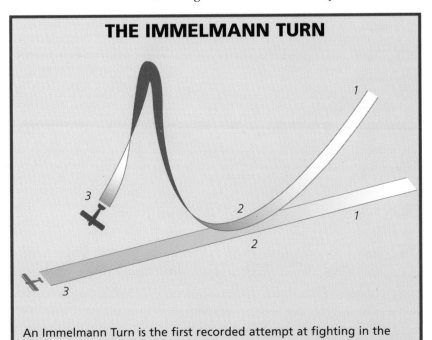

An Immelmann Turn is the first recorded attempt at fighting in the vertical rather than the horizontal plane. Speed from the initial diving attack was used to regain height while turning to reposition at the top of the climb.

Boelcke was the greatest tactical thinker of the war, of any nation. Working on empirical lines he analyzed each combat and arrived at reasoned conclusions. He compared the performance of his Fokker against that of his opponents using captured machines where possible. Gradually he evolved his rules for air fighting, the so-called Dicta Boelcke, stressing the advantages of height, position and surprise, and only firing at close range.

The majority of his opponents were artillery spotters or photographic machines which, by the very nature of their work, had their attention focused on the ground. The air threat at that time was minimal; in ten months of war, the RFC had fought only 46 air combats, most of which were inconclusive. This made their vulnerability to the new German fighter extreme, and many paid the ultimate price for not keeping a sharp lookout.

As Eindecker pilots gained confidence in their new mount, they began to score, slowly at first, then at an increasing tempo. With its monoplane wing, the Eindecker was relatively hard to see at any distance when approaching end-on, and this aided the element of surprise. Inexperienced in air combat, the RFC pilots found it difficult to defend against a fighter that could shoot forward through the propeller. The period that followed became known to the RFC as the "Fokker Scourge". Even to see one in the air was to be in mortal peril!

Objectively, the facts did not match the case. Not until the following year were Fokkers deployed in any numbers, while during 1915 the scoring rate of even the deadly duo of Boelcke and Immelmann barely exceeded one a month each! In absolute terms, RFC losses were small; only about 25 aircraft were lost in the final two months of 1915.

The slump in morale came from a feeling of helplessness.

The Vickers FB5 Gunbus was the first RFC fighter. Underpowered and unmaneuvrable, it was no match for the Eindecker. It was the first of a series of British pushers, and served in France from February 1915 until mid-1916.

The Airco DH2 was a single-seater pusher. Faster and more agile than the Eindecker, it was largely responsible for ending the Fokker Scourge. Its main fault was the unreliable Gnome Monosoupape engine. It was armed with a single fixed Lewis gun.

The lumbering RFC machines were no match for a fighter which could shoot through its propeller. Before long, three airplanes were needed to escort each reconnaissance machine or artillery spotter. While this reduced air combat losses, it resulted in an instant 75 per cent decrease in effectives. The cure was almost worse than the cause, at least from the point of view of the generals.

It is often stated that the first British fighter squadron arrived in France early in 1916. This was not in fact the case. The Vickers FB5 was an underpowered, two-seater pusher, which arrived at the front in February 1915. In July, 11 Squadron became the first unit to be entirely equipped with a single type of airplane and, by default, the first RFC fighter squadron.

Compared with the Eindecker, the FB5 was slow, had a lower ceiling, a slightly worse rate of climb (19 minutes to 6,500ft /1,980m), and was unmaneuvrable. Outperformed, it could not force the German machine to fight, nor could it easily break off the action. Seated in front of the pilot, the gunner had a clear field of fire ahead, but could offer no protection against attack from astern. Consequently the FB5 achieved little.

The ascendancy of the Fokker in the final months of 1915 spurred the British into action. The need for fighters able to defeat the Fokker, grouped in specialist fighting squadrons, was at last recognized. These started to arrive at the front in February 1916.

Although the tractor fighter with synchronization gear was the future, the British played safe and produced two new pushers. The Airco DH2 was a fast and agile single-seater, which handily outperformed the Eindecker in all departments. Its single Lewis gun was originally intended to swivel, but flying the airplane while aiming the gun was too much for one man, and it finally became fixed. The sole fault of the DH2 was an unreliable engine, which caused it to be dubbed "the spinning incinerator"!

The Royal Aircraft Factory produced the two-seater FE2b. Larger and more than twice as heavy as the DH2, its performance was broadly comparable to that of the Airco fighter, mainly due to a far more powerful engine. Two swivelling Lewis guns were fitted; one forward, the other on the top plane firing to the rear to give at least a modicum of defense against attack from astern. But to use the latter, the gunner stood precariously on his seat, with the cockpit coaming at ankle-level, to aim and fire. A safety strap was his sole insurance against falling overboard during his pilot's wilder gyrations.

Meanwhile the Aviation Militaire, which up to now had relied on deflectors, had come up with an alternative scheme. A fixed Lewis gun located on the top plane could fire straight ahead but over the top of the propeller. It was of course a problem that the Lewis was drum-fed. The standard drum held a mere 47 rounds, which meant that it had to be changed at frequent intervals. This was impossible in the middle of a fight, and no easy task at any time. Later, the problem was eased by using double drums, and a mounting that enabled the gun to be swung down for reloading. Introduced on the Nieuport 11 in the late summer of 1915, it was still in use at the end of the war.

The three Allied fighter types quickly wrested ascendancy away from the Eindecker, and after the death in action of Max Immelmann in June 1916, it faded from the scene.

FIGHTER DEVELOPMENT

The fact that the Eindecker was a monoplane was incidental. Almost every successful later fighter was a biplane, while two were actually triplanes, with three wings. Turning ability and rate of climb were largely dependent on the amount of lift that the wings could generate, and the biplane and triplane were more efficient in this respect, even though they suffered from greater profile drag, due to the larger frontal area. The two triplanes, the Sopwith and the

First introduced as a fighter in spring 1916, the FE.2 remained in the front line to the end of the war, although by then relegated to bombing and close air support. Here bombs are loaded onto an FE.2b of 142 Sqn in July 1918.

COMPARATIVE FIGHTER PERFORMANCE, 1917-1918

Type	Origin	Max.Speed mph (km/hr)	Rate of Climb	Ceiling (ft/m)
Nieuport 17	France	110/177	9min/9,843ft (3,000m)	17,390/5,300
SPAD S.7	France	119/191	6½ min/6,562ft (2,000m)	18,045/5,500
SPAD S.13	France	138/222	8min/9,843ft (3,000m)	21,819/6,650
Albatros D.III	Germany	108/174	4min/3,281ft (1,000m)	18,045/5,500
Fokker Dr.1	Germany	103/165	10min/13,124 ft(4,000m)	20,014/6,100
Fokker D.VII	Germany	135/217	16min/16,405 ft(5,000m)	22,967/7,000
Pfalz D.III	Germany	103/166	7min/9,843ft (3,000m)	17,061/5,200
Sopwith Pup	Gt Britain	111/179	10min/6,500ft (1,981m)	17,500/5,334
Sopwith Triplane	Gt Britain	116/187	10½min/10,000ft(3,048m)	20,500/6,248
Bristol F2b	Gt Britain	125/201	10min/6,500ft (1,981m)	20,000/6,096

NB. Speeds stated are at the best altitude, usually low. Rate of climb and ceiling are a better way of assessing relative fighting performance.

ROYAL AIRCRAFT FACTORY SE5a

Dimensions: Span 26ft 7½in (8.11m);
Length 20ft 11in (6.38m); Height 9ft 6in (2.90m);
Wing area 247sq.ft (22.95m²).
Power: One Wolseley Viper or Hispano inline engine
rated from 200-240hp.
Weights: Empty 1,387lb (629kg); Loaded 1,988lb(902kg).
Performance: Maximum speed 138mph (222km/hr);
Ceiling 19,500ft (5,943m); Climb 765ft/min (3.89m/sec);
Endurance 2½hr.
Armament: One fixed belt-fed Vickers machine gun; one
drum-fed Lewis gun firing over the top plane.
In Service: 1917/1918.

The SE5a was fast, climbed well, and was rugged and reliable. It entered service (as the SE5) in the spring of 1917, a time when the Royal Flying Corps was taking heavy losses to superior German fighters, and was largely responsible for reversing the situation. Although not the most agile of fighters, its outstanding performance, coupled with dive and zoom tactics, enabled it to more than hold its own. Its cockpit, although open, was relatively warm, which increased fighting efficiency. Many top-scoring RFC pilots, including Mannock, Bishop and McCudden, flew the SE5a.

Fokker Triplanes of Jasta 26.
The Dr I was not very fast, but extremely maneuvrable, and climbed rapidly.
Many German aces favored the type, while Manfred von Richthofen and Voss were both killed while flying the Dreidecker.

Fokker Dr.1, were extremely agile and climbed rapidly, but generally were not as speedy as their biplane counterparts.

The other major variation was the engine. The rotary, with a fixed crankshaft and cylinders which rotated around it, with the propeller bolted to them, was very compact, but lost power rapidly with increasing altitude. The inline, with a rotating crankshaft driving the propeller, and cylinders all in a row, was longer but heavier, mainly due to the coolant system with its associated radiator and plumbing. On

the other hand, it performed better than the rotary at high altitudes.

With the exception of the Dr.1, every major German fighter introduced after mid-1916 was an inline-engined biplane. The French stayed with the biplane, although the Nieuport series stayed with the rotary engine while SPADs used inlines. The British Sopwith company produced three outstanding rotary-powered fighters: the Scout (better known as the Pup); the Triplane, and the Biplane F.1 which was quickly dubbed the Camel. The Royal Aircraft Factory produced the superb inline-powered SE5a, and arguably the best of all, the Bristol F2B. This last was the only two-seater, but its 275hp Rolls-Royce Falcon engine enabled it to match the German single-seaters of the era. So good was the F2B that it remained in service until 1932! In action, the rotary-powered machines, with their weights clustered about the center of gravity, were the most maneuvrable; the inline-engined fighters performed better, especially at high altitudes. The Camel was the most agile fighter of the war, with an incredible rate of turn, but it was difficult to fly, and totally unforgiving of ham-fisted pilots.

PERFORMANCE VERSUS MANEUVRABILITY

One controversy never entirely resolved during the course of the war was which was the most important,

The SPAD S.7 was a rugged high performance fighter of only moderate maneuvrability. A French machine, it was also flown by the RFC, Italy and Russia. French aces who flew the SPAD S.7 included Guynemer, Fonck and Nungesser.

performance or maneuvrability. A feature of air fighting from 1917 onwards was the dogfight; a huge multi-bogey encounter with 50 or more participants. Typically it started with a flight of five or six engaging a similar number of enemy aircraft. From a distance, others would hasten to their aid until a large number of aircraft from both sides were involved.

In a dogfight, maneuvrability was all-important; the ability to bring sights to bear, or to turn out of the line of fire quickly. It was however a very dangerous place to be. The time taken to line up an opponent equally gave time for an opponent to take up an attacking position against ones' self. SE5a pilot Cecil Lewis of 56 Squadron noted ". . .most crack fighters did not get their victims in dogfights; they preferred safer means!" Sopwith Camel pilot Harold Balfour summed up the other view

with "Life on a Camel was certainly safer than on an SE, for though you could not be certain of your man, you could be reasonably sure of getting away if hard-pressed."

Performance conferred the ability to pick the moment to accept combat, preferably from a position of advantage, or to disengage at will. Maneuvrability only made the dogfight a slightly less dangerous place to be. Experience during the next few decades established performance as more desirable than maneuvrability. But in 1917/18 the issues were far less clear-cut.

THE RISE OF THE ACES

The ace fighter pilot was first recognized by the French and defined as a pilot who had shot down five enemy aircraft. The Germans were rather more conservative, dubbing those who had accounted for ten enemy aircraft as

SOPWITH CAMEL

Dimensions: Span 28ft 0in (8.53m); Length 18ft 9in (5.71m); Height 8ft 6in (2.59m); Wing area 231sq.ft (21.46m²).
Power: One 110hp Le Rhone, 130hp Clerget, 150hp Bentley BR 1, or 150hp Monosoupape rotary engine.
Weights: (150hp): Empty 962lb (436kg); Loaded 1,471lb(667kg).
Performance: 150hp: Maximum speed 121mph (195km/hr); Ceiling 20,000ft (6,096m); Climb 995ft/min(5.05m/sec); Endurance 2¼hr.
Armament: Two fixed belt-fed Vickers machine guns.
In Service: 1917/1918.

The Sopwith Camel was credited with destroying more enemy aircraft (1,294) than any other fighter of the war. On the other hand it was tricky to fly, and unforgiving of ham-fisted pilots. Because most of the weight was clustered centrally, inertia moments were small, making the Camel extremely responsive and maneuvrable. This was a tremendous advantage in the hurly-burly of the dogfight, both to get the sights on quickly for a shot, and to maneuver out of the line of fire of an assailant. On the other hand, the rotary engine lost power at altitude, reducing performance.

Top-scoring pilot Manfred von Richthofen comes in to land in his all-red (almost) Fokker Dr.I. His reasons for adopting this color are obscure, but it made him instantly identifiable in the air. Richthofen was an outstanding shot; his twin Spandaus were deadly.

Obercannone. The British never actually recognized the system at all, but this did not prevent the leading scorers being decorated at the front, and lionised and fêted when on leave.

As we saw earlier, the first German aces were Oswald Boelcke and Max Immelmann. Boelcke died after a mid-air collision with one of his own men in October 1916; his score 40. The "Father of Air Fighting", as he was dubbed, was the greatest of them all. He was eventually eclipsed by one of his pupils, the Red Baron, Manfred von Richthofen, who became the ranking ace with 80 victories. The second

highest scoring German was Ernst Udet, who survived the war.

One of the first French aces was Jean-Marie Navarre (12 victories), who flew an all-red Nieuport 11 over Verdun in 1916, thus predating the red fighter of Richthofen. He was eventually surpassed by Georges Guynemer (54 victories), a frail lad who was at first rejected for service in the Aviation Militaire. Guynemer was a leading exponent of the SPAD S.7 and flew with the elite Cigognes Escadrille. He vanished without trace in September 1917.

Albert Ball (44 victories) was the first high-

The name "Vieux Charles" instantly shows this to be the SPAD S.7 flown by Guynemer. Ernst Udet, who fought him on one occasion, commented "he anticipated all my moves!" A gifted pilot, Georges Guynemer became France's greatest air hero.

The greatest RFC ace of the early war was Albert Ball, seen here in the cockpit of his 56 Sqn SE.5. His specialty was to stalk enemy formations carefully, then attack from below from very close range. He was killed in a crash in May 1917.

scoring RFC pilot. The first "lone wolf" ace, his forte was to stalk enemy formations, then attack from below. Many of his victories were scored with the Nieuport, but he returned to France with 56 Squadron in April 1917 to fly the SE5. He crashed and died, probably after being disoriented in cloud, in May 1917.

Lone wolf aces were fairly common in 1916/17, but after that, with the accent on teamwork, their number declined. Billy Bishop and James McCudden specialized in hunting alone, but most of the later aces were, like Boelcke, fighter leaders. It is a fact that when Bishop relinquished command of 85 Squadron in 1918, its pilots rejected McCudden as his successor because they wanted a leader rather than a lone hunter. The choice then fell upon Edward Mannock, one of the greatest fighter leaders and tacticians of the war.

The top-scoring French ace was René Fonck (75 victories). A cool and patient character, he learned to spar around and wait until his opponent made a mistake. An outstanding marksman, he often accounted for a victim with only a handful of bullets. Although he handily outscored Guynemer, his methods were too clinical to catch the public imagination to any great extent.

While this was also the case with the Red Baron, Manfred von Richthofen, the latter is probably the best-known fighter pilot of all time. While his record is distinguished, he was in fact not a Baron, but a lower-ranking Freiherr. His fame stems from his all-red airplane, and that he led the brightly painted and numerically huge Richthofen Circus, Jagdgeschwader 1, comprising Jastas 4, 6, 10 and 11, as much as his final score of 80.

Although a pupil of Boelcke, Richthofen was not a great tactical innovator. An outstanding marksman, he is generally admitted to be inferior as an aircraft handler to Werner Voss, among others. He has been criticised for "picking on" vulnerable British two-seater artillery spotters rather than tackling single-seater scouts, but this is hardly fair. It was the airplanes which most aided the land forces which were the most valuable targets, and Richthofen fully recognized this. His choice was fully justified.

LEADING FIGHTER ACES OF WWI
(40 or more victories)

Name	Nationality	Score
Manfred von Richthofen	German	80
René Fonck	French	75
Edward Mannock	British	73
William Bishop	Canadian	72
Ernst Udet	German	62
Raymond Collishaw	Canadian	60
James McCudden	British	57
Georges Guynemer	French	54
A.Beauchamp-Proctor	South African	54
Donald MacLaren	Canadian	54
Erich Löwenhardt	German	53
William Barker	Canadian	52
Philip Fullard	British	52
Roderic Dallas	Australian	51
George McElroy	British	48
Werner Voss	German	48
Robert Little	Australian	47
Fritz Rumey	German	45
Albert Ball	British	44
Rudolf Berthold	German	44
Charles Nungesser	French	43
Paul Baumer	German	43
T.F.Hazell	British	41
H.J.Larkin	British	41
Bruno Lörzer	German	41
Josef Jacobs	German	41
Georges Madon	French	41
Ira Jones	British	40
Oswald Boelcke	German	40
Franz Büchner	German	40
Lothar von Richthofen	German	40

Between the Wars

1918-1939

The two-seater Bristol F2B was powered by a Rolls-Royce Falcon engine of 275hp, which enabled it to be handled like a single-seater in combat. It remained in service long after World War I; this example of 31 Sqn is seen over the North-West Frontier of India in 1930.

THE GREAT WAR had made the advanced nations air-minded, and the two decades that followed saw tremendous advances in engine and airplane design. But with the end of "the war to end all wars", the emphasis was on peaceful usage. Pioneering flights, firstly across the Atlantic, then across the rest of the world, received most of the headlines. The accent was on reliability, range, and load-carrying. For several years fighter design was neglected, and the few airplanes that managed to enter service over the next decade performed little better than their wartime predecessors. This was hardly surprising; Germany, the major threat, had been crushed, and with no real threat to counter there was little incentive for fighter development.

There was however an incentive to produce better and faster airplanes. Speed competitions, the best known of which were the Gordon Bennett Cup for landplanes, and the Schneider Trophy for seaplanes, were a source of national pride. To win them, or even better, to set a new absolute speed record, was to gain prestige for the successful nation. In particular, the Schneider Trophy did much to stimulate high-speed flight, both in engine and airframe design.

THE POWER TO FIGHT

In 1919, the two basic types of fighter engines were the water-cooled inline, and the air-cooled rotary. The former was longer, although the adoption of a Vee-shaped configuration held this within reasonable bounds. It was also intrinsically heavier, even without taking into account the weight of the radiator, plumbing and coolant. The latter also made it more vulnerable to battle damage; loss of coolant quickly caused it to overheat and seize up. To counter this disadvantage, the inline had a smaller frontal area, with less drag, while power did not fall away with altitude at the same rate as it did with the rotary. The fighters of the Great War with the highest performance were all powered by inline engines.

The rotary was shorter and lighter, but because the cylinders were spread out around it, frontal area, and therefore drag, were high. In addition, getting fuel and ignition to a bank of cylinders which were frantically whirling around the central fixed crankshaft, was far from easy. This meant that it could not be throttled; it ran flat out or not at all. To reduce speed, the ignition could be cut with a thumb switch, but this was the only means of control.

The eventual answer was the radial engine. This retained the compact layout of the rotary, and was also aircooled, making it relatively light. In the radial engine, the cylinders remained stationary, and only the crankshaft, driven by connecting rods from the pistons, moved to turn the propeller. Also it could be throttled, giving far greater speed control. It still had a greater frontal area than an inline, but the drag from this was largely offset by the saving in weight.

Peacetime speed contests, notably the Schneider Trophy, did much to further airplane performance. Seen here is the Supermarine S.5 taking off from Calshot on its first test flight in 1927. This particular machine was a back-up which did not compete.

The radial engine had been designed before 1914, but the rush to produce military aircraft had delayed its development. Traditionally, engines always take longer to develop than airframes, and the radial was no exception. One of its first service uses was, in the form of the Armstrong Siddeley Jaguar, powering the Nieuport Nighthawk in 1920. The relative simplicity and light weight of the radial engine makes it significant that, with only one exception, every biplane fighter flown by the Royal Air Force (as the Royal Flying Corps had become in 1918) over the next two decades was radial-engined.

Whilst the radial engine was the most radical advance of the immediate post-war years, general engine technology did not stand still. Between 1925 and 1935 engine power increased by about 50 per cent. At the same time, engine weight per horsepower fell by more than 20 per cent, and fuel consumption per horsepower was reduced by about the same amount.

The next event in engine development was supercharging. Without this, power tended to fall away as air pressure (and its oxygen content) reduced with altitude. In fact, legend had it that the Kestrel engine of the Hawker Hart biplane bomber, which entered service in 1930, gave so

The Supermarine S.6B which in 1931 won the Schneider Trophy for Britain. This airplane was a direct ancestor of the Spitfire, while its Rolls-Royce engine led to the development of the superb Merlin.

In the early '30s the Bristol Bulldog was the numerically most important fighter of the RAF. The Bristol Jupiter radial engine provided a maximum speed of 174mph (280km/hr) and a ceiling of 27,000ft (8,229m). It was armed with two .303 Vickers machine guns.

little power at 18,000ft(5,486m) that it used hardly any fuel, and would therefore fly forever!

Supercharging was a method of compressing air as it entered the engine, to give greater pressure, increasing power as it did so. This effectively gave aircraft far better performance at high altitude. Still later, two-stage supercharging and turbocharging was introduced, pushing operational ceilings up towards the stratosphere. This was combined with ever-higher octane fuels; fuel development played an important part in increasing engine power during these years.

Propeller design was the final stage in increasing power. All early aircraft had fixed-pitch propellers, which were at their most efficient mid-way in the speed range. At the bottom end (takeoff) and the top end (maximum speed) they operated well below maximum efficiency, laboring at low speeds, or with the engine overspeeding at the top end of the range. To overcome this, pitch was made variable. At first only two settings were used; fine pitch for takeoff and coarse pitch for economical cruising, but shortly before the Second World War automatic variable pitch was introduced, giving an optimum setting for speed and altitude. But not until the war was well underway did the variable-pitch propeller become standard.

AERODYNAMICS AND STRUCTURES

More powerful and efficient engines were only part of the story of the search for increased performance. The other side of the coin was to decrease aerodynamic drag. Weight reduction was of less importance, and in fact performance could often be increased by trading increased weight for reduced drag. The prime example of this was the retractable undercarriage, which with its hydraulics and general structural stiffening was considerably heavier than its fixed counterpart. However, the extra weight was

POLIKARPOV I-16 Type 17

Dimensions: Span 29ft 6¾in (9.01m);
Length 20ft 1in (6.12m); Height 8ft 5in (2.57m);
Wing area 1611/2sq.ft (15m²).
Power: One Shvetsov M-25V radial engine rated at 750hp.
Weights: Empty 3,296lb (1,495kg);
Loaded 3,990lb(1,810kg).
Performance: Maximum speed 264mph (425km/hr);
Ceiling 25,920ft (7,900m); Climb 61/2min/16,405ft (5,000m); Range 401 miles (645km).
Armament: Two 20mm ShVAK cannon and two 7.72mm ShKAS machine guns.
In service: 1934/1942.

The I-16 was the first monoplane fighter with a cantilever wing, a retractable undercarriage, an enclosed cockpit, and armor protection for the pilot. It was therefore the fore-runner of the World War II generation of fighters. The combat debut of the I-16 came in the Spanish Civil War during the winter of 1936/37, and it was also used by Russia against Japan in the Nomonghan Incident in 1938. Although obsolescent when Germany invaded Russia in 1941, in one area it was never surpassed. The original I-16 had carried two 7.62 machine guns; two 20mm ShVAK cannon were added to the Type 17, giving it an exceptionally heavy weight of fire.

more than offset by the reduction in drag, leading to improved performance.

The main feature to be dropped in the quest for aerodynamic efficiency was the biplane configuration. This had been retained for many years as giving a large wing area (lift) combined with a fairly small span (roll rate and climb), for maneuvrability. Whereas performance had been rated higher than maneuvrability in the Great War, the distinction was not clear-cut. Post-war thinking and developments made this rather more obvious.

The quest for performance led inevitably to the monoplane. The Boeing P-26 Peashooter featured braced wings and a fixed undercarriage with "trousers", but the exactly contemporary Russian Polikarpov I-16 was of cantilevered construction with a retractable undercarriage and an enclosed cockpit. As such it was the first modern fighter of its day. Later variants of the I-16 became for a while the most heavily armed fighter in the world.

Monocoque metal construction was the next step, saving structural weight. Inevitably, monoplanes were higher wing-loaded than their biplane counterparts, and in consequence could not turn as tightly, even though their rate of roll might be better. The other factor was liquid-cooled inline versus air-cooled radial engines. In terms of drag, the inline won every time, whereas if weight was the main consideration, the radial held the advantage. By 1939, most fighters were powered by inline engines.

INTERNATIONAL OVERVIEW

For many nations, the greatest problem was in deciding what the balance of their air force ought to be. Should it be mainly tactical, for the support of the ground forces; or should it have a significant strategic component? Much depended on the world role of the individual nation, its treaty commitments and vested interests, geography and, hardest of all to predict, threats. But what really confused the issue was the predicted future of strategic bombing.

Usually regarded as the "halfway-house" fighter between the two World Wars, the Boeing P-26 Peashooter was the first American monoplane fighter. Radial-engined, with fixed "trousered" wheels and wire-braced wings, it fought in the Philippines against the Japanese in 1941.

Developed from the Curtiss P-1 Hawk, the P-6E took the biplane configuration almost as far as it would go. This machine is from the 17th Pursuit Squadron, USAAC, based at Selfridge Field, Michigan.

Fitting two 20mm Hispano cannon into the wing of a Spitfire was a tight squeeze and, as seen here, they had to be staggered. Ammunition tanks are also staggered one behind the other.

Strategic bombing had commenced during the Great War, and while this had been far from decisive, it influenced post-war thinking to a disproportionate extent. The theory was that the bomber would always get through; and that directed against the war-making potential of a nation, its destructive power made it potentially a war-winning weapon. The theory was quite correct, only assuming that the postulated levels of destruction could be achieved. It took the Second World War to prove that they could not, and that the concept was beyond the technology of the day.

Bomber performance in the Great War had been rather less than that of fighters, but even then interception had been problematical. The advances in engine and airframe technology in the 1920s and 1930s improved bomber performance to the point where interception became very difficult, if not impossible. The result was that bombers appeared in many ways to be far more decisive instruments of war than fighters, the development of which languished.

When in the 1930s a resurgent Germany began to pose a possible threat, Britain took two active measures. The first, to which a great deal of the defense budget was allocated, was to build up the strategic bomber force as a deterrent. The second was to find a way of making the fighter defense effective.

With the bomber as the primary target, the priorities for fighter design changed. Whereas in the Great War fighters had to be able to hold their own in maneuver combat with other fighters,

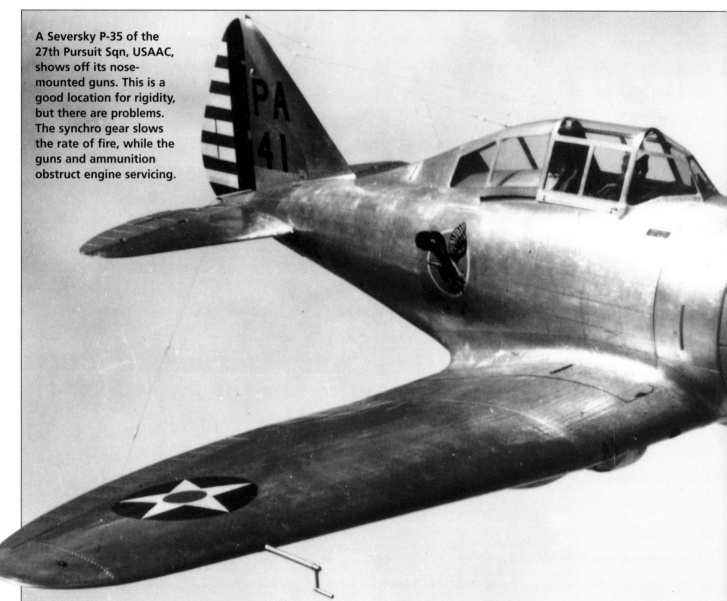

A Seversky P-35 of the 27th Pursuit Sqn, USAAC, shows off its nose-mounted guns. This is a good location for rigidity, but there are problems. The synchro gear slows the rate of fire, while the guns and ammunition obstruct engine servicing.

bomber interception was a very different matter. Performance now became all-important; maximum speed, rate of climb and ceiling, all were increased, at the expense of maneuvrability.

WEAPONRY

Against the wood and canvas airplanes of the Great War, a single rifle-caliber machine gun had been found inadequate, and two guns had become the norm. Against the much tougher monoplane bombers that entered service from the mid-1930s, this was demonstrably insufficient. The solution was to use bigger guns and/or more of them.

The ideal place for mounting aircraft guns was still in the nose, firing more or less along the axis of the airplane. The mounting could be made much more rigid, with the recoil forces transmitted directly to the main structure. There were however two disadvantages. The first was synchronization to miss the propeller blades, which reduced the rate of fire, typically by 10 per cent. The second was that the number of guns which could be mounted around the engine was very limited.

Even as engine and airframe design had advanced, so had gun design. Reliability had been greatly improved, to the point where gun jams were rare. This meant that it was no longer necessary to have the breeches within reach of the pilot. Now the guns could safely be located in the wings and fired remotely, with no loss of firing rate due to synchronization. The only problem was that the recoil could cause the wings to flex slightly, particularly in maneuvring flight. This gave a small scattering effect, but as the average pilot was not much of a marksman this made little difference in combat.

The most important parameters of fighter guns are projectile weight, rate of fire, and muzzle velocity. The larger the projectile, the more destructive it is. The higher the rate of fire, the more hits are likely to be scored in a quick burst. The higher the muzzle velocity, the greater the effective range and aiming accuracy, although this is modified by the ballistic qualities of the projectile.

Air-to-air gunnery thus becomes a tradeoff between the number of hits and destructive power. The Royal Air Force were at one extreme; their new breed of monoplane fighters carried eight 7.7mm Browning machine guns in the wings, which could pour out an average of 153 rounds per second, giving a very high bullet density. By contrast, the 20mm Oerlikon MGFF cannon widely used by Germany could pump out only slightly fewer than six shells a second; two MGFFs were generally carried, plus two engine-mounted 7.9mm machine guns. Thus the British fighters were almost ten times more likely to score hits, although the hits were much less damaging than the 20mm. The United States standardized on the 12.7mm heavy machine gun as their primary fighter weapon, and this served them well for the next two decades. The almost optimum shape of the 12.7 projectile made for excellent performance.

The thick wing of the Hurricane allowed easy installation of two 20mm Hispano cannon and their ammunition tanks. The firepower of the Hurricane IIc could tear up any enemy airplane in short order.

Heinkel He 51s of JG 2 Richthofen. Sent to Spain as part of the Kondor Legion, the He 51 was quickly outclassed by Russian-built I-15s and I-16s, and relegated to bombing and close air support duties.

AIMING THE GUNS

Fixed ring and bead sights had been standard for much of the Great War, followed by the Aldiss telescopic sight, but the restricted view through the latter tended to give the pilot target fixation. The reflector sight was introduced during the 1930s. This carried a circle of light and a central aiming dot projected on to a glass screen in front of the pilot. Focused at infinity, this enabled the pilot to aim, and still be aware of what else was happening in front of him. Several air forces, including the USAAC, retained the ring and bead as a backup in case the reflector sight failed.

SMALL WARS

The Spanish Civil War broke out in 1936. Germany and Italy, the two Fascist dictatorships, offered military assistance to General Franco's Nationalist forces, while Russian "volunteers" flying Polikarpov I-15 biplanes and I-16 monoplanes, arrived to help the Republicans. The air war was essentially tactical in nature, and air superiority and close air support were the main requirements.

The German Heinkel He 51 was outclassed by the two Russian fighters; only the superb maneuvrability and slightly greater firepower (two 12.7mm Breda-SAFAT machine guns) of the Italian CR.32 allowed it to meet them on something approaching equal terms. The one thing that neither side was able to do effectively was to intercept the fast monoplane bombers then in service: the Russian SB-2; the German He 111 and Do 17, and the Italian SM.79. Interceptions occasionally happened, but they were largely a matter of luck.

SCHWARM FORMATION

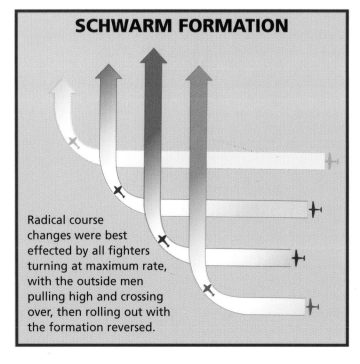

Radical course changes were best effected by all fighters turning at maximum rate, with the outside men pulling high and crossing over, then rolling out with the formation reversed.

CROSS-OVER TURN

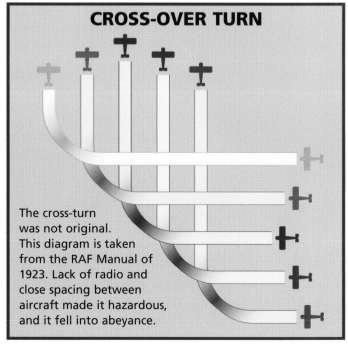

The cross-turn was not original. This diagram is taken from the RAF Manual of 1923. Lack of radio and close spacing between aircraft made it hazardous, and it fell into abeyance.

FIAT CR.32

Dimensions: Span 31ft 2in (9.50m);
Length 24ft 3½ in (7.40m); Height 8ft 7½ in (2.63m);
Wing area 238sq.ft (22.10m²).
Power: One Fiat A30RA inline engine
rated at 600hp.
Weights: Empty 3,208lb (1,445kg);
Loaded 4,222lb (1,915kg).
Performance: Maximum speed 221mph (355km/hr);
Ceiling 25,264ft (7,700m); Climb 14.42min/19,686ft
(7,700m); Range 485 miles (780km).
Armament: Two 12.7mm Breda-SAFAT machine guns
(375 rounds each).
In service: 1933/1941.

Biplane fighters reigned supreme from 1916 to the mid-1930s. The Italian Fiat CR.32 was one of the finest fighters in the world when it entered service in 1933. Its combat debut came in 1936 in the Spanish Civil War, where it was fairly successful against the Russian-designed and flown fighters of the Republican forces.

Top-scorer Garcia Morato flew the CR.32. Unfortunately Spanish experience led the Italians to the conclusion that maneuvrability was the prime asset of a fighter, and the CR.32 was superseded by the CR.42; also a biplane. A few CR.32s saw action in 1940.

In the spring of 1937, the Messerschmitt Me 109 arrived in Spain. Prior to this, fighters of both persuasions flew in Vics of three or five airplanes, in close formation so that all could see the leader's hand signals.

An initial shortage of '109s made this impossible, and instead they flew in pairs. The then innovation of air-to-air radio enabled them to fly widely spaced, typically at about 600ft (183m) apart. It was soon realized that this was a better tactical system, and as numbers increased they flew in a Schwarm of four airplanes, all covering each other's blind spots below and astern. At this point the future German ace Werner Mölders arrived on the scene.

One of the problems of formations with a wide frontage was maintaining position in a radical turn. To overcome this, Mölders introduced the cross-over turn, in which all airplanes turned at the maximum rate, reversing positions in the formation as they did so. It is often stated that Mölders invented the pair and the crossover turn, but in fact both were predated by many years, and probably originated in 1918 if not earlier.

The Russians copied the four and the crossover, even though they had no air-to-air radio. But when they returned to their homeland, most of the leaders vanished in Stalin's purges, and the lessons of Spain were forgotten.

Russia was also involved in the Far East at this time. A war between China and Japan had been going on intermittently for some time, with the latter triumphant in the air. Russia aided the Chinese, and ferocious air battles took place in 1937 and 1938.

Japanese fighters were designed for maneuvrability above all else and, while this made them formidable opponents, the Russians had learned to use dive and zoom tactics in Spain against the agile Fiats. By now they had

the I-16 type 17, armed with two 20mm cannon in addition to its machine guns, and with 9mm armor protection for the pilot. A couple of 20mm hits was enough to blow the unprotected Japanese fighters apart, while the I-16s could absorb a considerable amount of damage from the 7.7mm Japanese machine guns. The admitted losses of both sides during four months fighting were 207 Russians, 168 Japanese. But like the Spanish Civil War, the Chinese battles were a sideshow. The big one was still to come.

Examination of this picture shows that unusually for a biplane, the Russian Polikarpov I-153 had retractable main gears. The type was used extensively in the Spanish Civil War on the Republican side.

The Messerschmitt Me 109 made its debut in the Spanish Civil War. An initial shortage of aircraft led to the pair being adopted as the basic fighting unit, and fortuitously the Germans developed a whole new tactical doctrine as an indirect result.

War in the West

1939-1943

The last British biplane fighter was the Gloster Gladiator. Armed with four .303 machine guns, it also featured an enclosed cockpit. In World War II it did well against Italian biplane fighters, but was out-classed by the new monoplane generation.

FROM THE MID-1930S it became increasingly clear that Germany was bent on a policy of aggressive expansion. The new Luftwaffe had become a large and apparently efficient force, and to Britain and France, the major democracies in Western Europe, increasingly posed a threat. A major European war had become merely a question of time, although no-one could see how vast it would eventually become. The pot came to the boil in September 1939 when Poland was invaded, and Britain and France honored their guarantees to her sovereignty and declared war on Germany.

There is rarely a good time for an international crisis. In France, l'Armée de l'Air was numerically strong but, with a large proportion of obsolescent airplanes, was caught in the middle of a huge re-equipment program. But whatever their failings, the French, lulled into a state of false security by the supposedly impregnable defenses of the Maginot Line, were at least prepared to fight a mainly tactical air war.

The same could not be said of the British. The RAF was busy building up a strategic bomber force, while its fighter squadrons re-equipped with the new eight-gun monoplanes, Hurricanes and Spitfires. Fighter Command had in fact equipped and trained for the wrong war. The projected threat consisted of large fleets of unescorted bombers heading in over the North Sea, and virtually all Fighter Command's tactics and training had been planned to counter this. There was however a degree of flexibility in the service as a whole; the RAF had a considerable force of light bombers. With the outbreak of war several squadrons of these were despatched to France, with fighters to protect them.

Over the next few months, air activity along the Franco-German border consisted mainly of skirmishes. Neither side was willing to escalate the war by bombing targets in the enemy

At the outbreak of war, the most numerous French fighter was the Morane-Saulnier MS.406. Performance was inferior to that of the Me 109E, mainly due to the low-powered Hispano engine. Armament consisted of two wing-mounted 7.5mm machine guns and a 20mm engine-mounted cannon.

homeland, for fear of retaliation in kind, with heavy civilian casualties. Effectively the only legitimate objectives were naval assets located well away from civilian areas.

The first theory to be disproved was that close formations of unescorted bombers could defend themselves against fighter attack. On December 14 1939, 12 Wellington bombers fitted with powered gun turrets attacked German shipping in the Jade Estuary. Intercepted by German fighters, they lost five of their number. Two days later, 22 Wellingtons were intercepted. Twelve were shot down and two more crashed on return. This loss rate could not be sustained. The fighter had won the first round; from this point, the RAF switched to night bombing.

THE FRENCH CAMPAIGN

The relative calm of the Franco-German front was broken on May 10 1940. The German army turned the northern flank of the Maginot Line by the simple expedient of violating Dutch and Belgian neutrality and, spearheaded by close air support units of the Luftwaffe, swept into France. The small Dutch and Belgian air forces were quickly swept aside, and were mainly destroyed on the ground. At the same time, bombing raids were mounted against French airfields and communications centers.

French and British fighters put up a fierce resistance, but were handicapped by the lack of an effective early warning and control system. Rarely were they able to be in the right place at the right time. They were also heavily outnumbered; l'Armée de l'Air had 552 relatively modern fighters, of which just over half were Morane-Saulnier MS.406s. The RAF fighters consisted of just four Hurricane squadrons, later reinforced with six more, and two squadrons of obsolescent Gladiator biplanes. Against these were ranged 860 Me 109 single-engined and 350 twin-engined Me 110 fighters, to protect 1,680 level and dive bombers.

The fashion for long-range fighters saw several twin-engined designs emerge, of which the Messerschmitt Me 110 was the best. Heavy and unmaneuvrable, it was far too vulnerable in combat with single-seat single-engined fighters.

The most advanced British trainer of the early war years was the Miles Master, seen here flown by American Eagle Squadron members. The fighter-like appearance and handling of the Master made it ideal for the task.

The Luftwaffe held two tremendous advantages. The first was the initiative, which generally enabled it to be in the right place at the right time in sufficient force. The second was the speed of the Wehrmacht's advance into France, which threatened to overrun Allied airfields. British and French fighter units were forced to retreat, often to emergency landing grounds with poor or non-existent communications. The French early warning system collapsed, supply systems disintegrated, and fighting effectiveness diminished in consequence. Two other factors signally contributed to the defeat of the Allied fighters.

The basic fighter element of the British and French was the three-ship Vic, or patrouille. The British were trained to hold very close formation, partly as an effective way of penetrating the cloud-laden skies of their native island without losing integrity, and partly because it squared with the close order drill of their standard attacks on unescorted bombers. Most pilots were too busy holding formation to keep an effective lookout, which made them vulnerable to surprise attack. While some squadrons copied the French system of weavers, with two or three airplanes flying above and behind the main formation to guard its tail, in practice it was found that weavers were generally the first to be picked off.

TURNING ABILITY

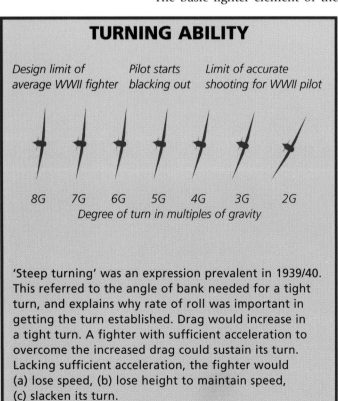

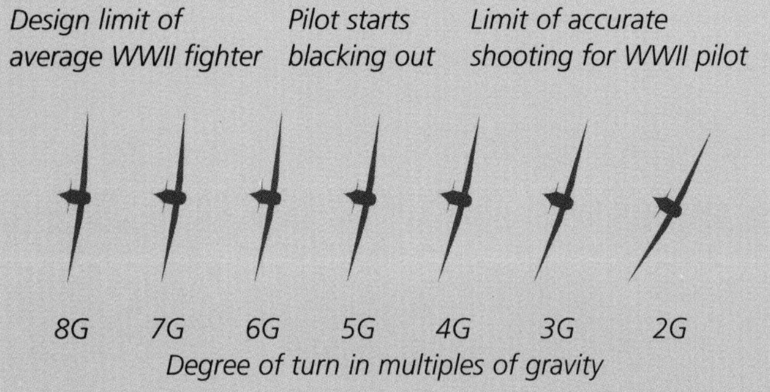
Design limit of average WWII fighter
Pilot starts blacking out
Limit of accurate shooting for WWII pilot
8G
7G
6G
5G
4G
3G
2G
Degree of turn in multiples of gravity

'Steep turning' was an expression prevalent in 1939/40. This referred to the angle of bank needed for a tight turn, and explains why rate of roll was important in getting the turn established. Drag would increase in a tight turn. A fighter with sufficient acceleration to overcome the increased drag could sustain its turn. Lacking sufficient acceleration, the fighter would (a) lose speed, (b) lose height to maintain speed, (c) slacken its turn.

STAFFEL FORMATION

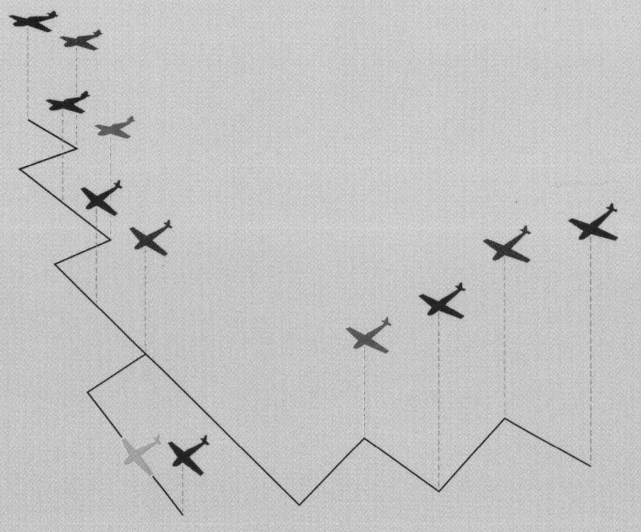

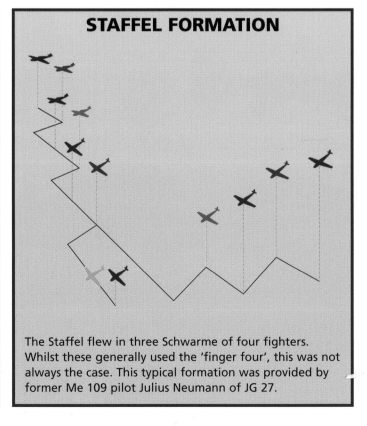

The Staffel flew in three Schwarme of four fighters. Whilst these generally used the 'finger four', this was not always the case. This typical formation was provided by former Me 109 pilot Julius Neumann of JG 27.

MESSERSCHMITT Me 109E

Dimensions: Span 32ft 4in (9.85m);
Length 28ft 4in (8.63m);
Height 11ft 2in (3.40m);
Wing area 174sq.ft (16.16m²).
Power: One Daimler-Benz DB601A
liquid-cooled V-12 rated at 1,100hp.
Weights: Empty 4,421lb (2,005kg);
Loaded 5,523lb (2,505kg).
Performance: Maximum speed 354mph
(570km/hr); Ceiling 36,091ft (11,000m);
Climb 6min 12sec to 16,405ft (5,000m);
Range 412 miles (663km).
Armament: Two nose-mounted 7.92mm
MG17 machine guns with 1,000 rounds
per gun, and two wing-mounted 20mm
MGFF cannon with 60 rounds per gun.

First flown in August 1935, the Me 109
made its combat debut in Spain, and
became the main German fighter of
World War II, with about 35,000 produced of all types.
Like its great rival the Spitfire, it was progressively up-
gunned and up-engined, but the extra weight adversely
affected its handling qualities, which had never been
particularly benign. Losses in takeoff and landing accidents were high. This apart, it was a worthy
opponent in the right hands, and virtually all the high-
scoring Luftwaffe aces flew it at one time or another.
Ranking ace Erich Hartmann (352 victories on the
Eastern Front) flew nothing else.

The French three-ship patrouille was more of
a fighting formation, with a frontage of about
600ft (182m) and airplanes stepped vertically by
160ft (50m). To guard against the surprise
bounce out of the sun, the lowest man was
stationed on this side. This notwithstanding, the
patrouille still contained one airplane too many.

The basic two-ship German element, or
Rötte, with a leader and wingman, and two
Rötten making up a Schwarm, was tactically
superior, mainly because it was far more
flexible, while the Jagdflieger, experienced and
battle-hardened in Spain and Poland, were
tactically far more advanced.

The second factor was that in the air the Allied
fighters were generally outnumbered. The reason
for this came from the basic organizations of the
respective air forces. Normal flying strength of an
RAF fighter squadron was 12 airplanes. Only
rarely did they try to combine into wings of up
to three squadrons, and because they had never
trained for this, the larger formation was
inflexible and vulnerable.

The basic French fighter formation was the
Group de Chasse composed of two or three
Escadrilles of about a dozen airplanes each. In
practice they tended to fly in individual
Escadrilles.

The basic German fighter unit was the
Gruppe, composed of three Staffeln and a Stab
(staff flight). When Messerschmitts were on the
prowl, they were often encountered in
formations of 30 or more, with individual
Staffeln supporting each other. Against the
smaller British and French units, this gave them
a considerable numerical advantage.

The Me 109E was undoubtedly the best fighter
of the French campaign. It was fast, climbed and
accelerated well, and carried 20mm cannon
armament, even though this was the Oerlikon
MGFF, with a low muzzle velocity and poor rate
of fire. It had a fuel-injected engine rather than
carburation, which enabled it to stuff its nose
down and pull negative-g without its engine
cutting, a maneuver which Allied fighters could
follow only by rolling inverted and pulling
through, losing ground in the process.

Werner Mölders, the leading scorer in Spain,
retained his lead with a further 25 victories,
although on June 5 1940 he was shot down by
a Dewoitine D.520 and taken prisoner.
Unfortunately for the British he was freed after
the French surrender three weeks later. Wilhelm
Balthasar, who had scored seven in Spain, ran
him close in France with 23 victories, including
nine in one day on June 6.

The late 1930s had seen a fashion emerge for
twin-engined long range fighters, of which the
German Me 110 was the best. Although heavily

**Preparing for war!
A German 'black man',
so called for the color
of his overalls, carries
out a thorough check
on the Daimler-Benz
DB 601 engine of an
Me 109E. Pilots relied
on the quality of
servicing, especially
on overwater flights.**

Hurricane Is at the Cowley Repair Depot prior to reissue to the squadrons. Badly damaged aircraft were trucked to the depot and rebuilt. During the Battle of Britain, one Hurricane was shot down three times and rebuilt on each occasion.

armed with two 20mm MGFF cannon and four 7.9mm machine guns in the nose, and a swivelling machine gun for rear defense, it lacked performance and agility. Successful in Poland, it was outclassed by modern single-seaters. When attacked Me 110 units adopted the defensive circle, in which the tail of the preceding airplane was covered by the one behind it. While this was difficult for its opponents to crack, it was hardly offensive either.

The best Allied fighter of this period was the

Hurricane. Although of lower performance than the '109, its lower wing loading enabled it to out-turn the latter with ease, while at close range its battery of eight machine guns could inflict horrendous damage. Described by RAF ace Jim Lacey, it was "a collection of non-essential parts", which enabled it to sustain heavy battle damage and survive. Leading Hurricane aces in France were Fanny Orton with 17 and Cobber Kain with 16 victories.

The best French fighter of the period was the Dewoitine D.520, although it was available only in small numbers. Top scorer with the D.520 was Pierre LeGloan who, flying against the Italians in June 1940, scored seven victories. French top scorers of the campaign were Edmond Marin la Meslée with 15, and Michel Dorance and Camille Plubeau with 14 each, all of whom flew the American-built Curtiss Hawk 75A.

The radial-engined Hawk 75A, armed with one 12.7mm and three 7.62mm machine guns, was not the best-performing fighter around, but at high speed its finely harmonized controls made it the best handling of them all. It was also the only airplane in the theater fitted with an automatic constant-speed variable pitch propeller, which enabled its engine to run at maximum efficiency throughout the speed range. On one notable occasion, nine Hawks were bounced by a whole Gruppe of Me 109Ds led by Hannes Gentzen, top-scorer in Poland. The French fought back fiercely and shot down four '109s, while another four '109s force-landed. Their own losses, at adverse odds of 3:1, was a single repairable Hawk.

As the Wehrmacht raced across France, the air campaign was lost on the ground. Command and logistics disintegrated as airfield after airfield was overrun, and the British army was driven back on Dunkirk. There, for the first time, the Luftwaffe came within reach of British-based fighters, and also for the first time Me 109s encountered the Spitfire.

The latter came as a nasty shock to the Jagdflieger; its performance was very similar to that of the Me 109E, while its manoeuvrability was far superior. Hard fighting took place; but again the RAF was at a disadvantage. Operating far from their bases, they were only able to stay on station for a very limited time, and when they were there, their targets were the bombers. This, plus the out-dated RAF tactics of the

The best French fighter of the war was the Dewoitine D.520 as seen here. Unfortunately only a few took part in the French campaign. It was armed with one 20mm cannon and four 7.5mm machine guns.

DAY FIGHTER PERFORMANCE COMPARISONS
WESTERN FRONT 1939-43

Type	Origin	Max.Speed mph(km/hr)	Rate of Climb	Ceiling (ft/m)
MS.406	France	304/490	9min 3sec to 19,686ft/6,000m	32,810/10,000
Hurricane I	Britain	316/508	8min 30sec to 20,000ft/6,096m	33,200/10,119
Spitfire V	Britain	374/602	7min 30sec to 20,000ft/6,096m	37,000/11,277
Me 109F	Germany	391/629	6min to 19,868ft/6,096m	39,372/12,000
Spitfire IX	Britain	408/657	6min 46sec to 20,000ft/6,096m	44,000/13,411
Me 109G	Germany	387/623	6min to 19,868ft/6,000m	38,551/11,750
Hawk 75A	USA/France	311/500	4min 54sec to 15,000ft/4,572m	32,700/9,966

period, saw British fighter losses exceed those of the Germans by a considerable margin. Total losses of all types were 106 British and 92 German. Some 55 of the latter were bombers.

THE BATTLE OF BRITAIN

In July 1940 Britain stood alone. A few miles away, across the gray waters of the English Channel, lay the world's mightiest air force, flushed with victory. Prewar, Fighter Command had prepared to meet an onslaught by massive formations of unescorted bombers. This was no longer the case; the bombers could now be escorted by single-seater fighters. The odds had

lengthened immeasurably, but Fighter Command RAF had one last card to play. Well before the war, an integrated detection, command and control system had been set up.

From a chain of radar stations around the coast, invisible electronic beams searched the air far out to sea, and where the Channel was narrowest, deep into France. They could detect airplanes more than 100 miles(160km) distant and give accurate range and course indications. Indications of heights and numbers were less accurate. Inland behind the radar screen lay a network of observer posts, each reporting in to a control center. Here the information from radar

The Curtiss Hawk 75 was flown by three of the top-scoring French aces in 1940. Finely harmonized controls made it a delight to handle, and it was the only airplane in France 1940 to have a constant-speed propeller. This machine is an RAF Mohawk IV.

SUPERMARINE SPITFIRE I

Dimensions: Span 36ft 10in (11.23m); Length 29ft 11in (9.12m); Height 11ft 5in (3.48m); Wing area 242sq.ft (22.48m^2).
Power: One Rolls-Royce Merlin liquid-cooled V-12 rated at 1,030hp.
Weights: Empty 4,810lb (2,182kg); Loaded 5,784lb (2,624kg).
Performance: Maximum speed 355mph (571km/hr); Ceiling 34,000ft (10,363m); Climb 6min 12sec to 15,000ft(4,572m); Range 575miles (925km).
Armament: Eight wing-mounted 7.62mm Colt Browning machine guns with 300 rounds each.

First flown in March 1936, the Spitfire entered large-scale service just in time for World War II. Over Dunkirk in 1940, and during the Battle of Britain, it established a reputation second to none, and its ability to hold tight turns was outstanding. Later models were fitted with progressively more powerful engines and cannon armament, and such was the excellence of the original design that development continued until the end of the war, by this time with the more advanced Griffon engine. It served in every theater of the war, was tropicalized for desert and jungle, and navalized for carrier operations as the Seafire. It is widely regarded as the greatest fighter of the war.

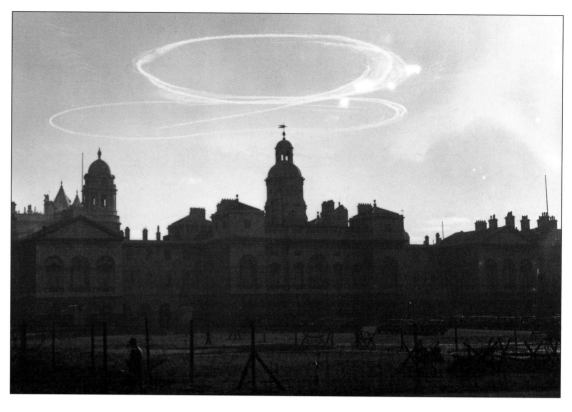

Contrails high over London on October 8 1940 as British fighters intercept a high-flying fighter-bomber raid by Me 109Es. Feldwebel Boche of 4/JG 52 was posted missing after this encounter.

Scramble! Pilots of 610 Squadron race to their Spitfires. Even seconds were vital, and each minute wasted was over 2,000ft (609m) of altitude lost. In World War II, even more than in the First, altitude was the primary advantage.

stations and observer posts was analyzed, German raids were tracked and plotted, and fighter squadrons were scrambled to intercept. By modern standards the reporting system was crude and inaccurate; in the summer of 1940 it proved just good enough. It allowed the British fighters to be more or less where they were wanted, more or less when they were wanted.

The Battle of Britain was actually a campaign, with minor skirmishes on some days and major engagements on others. The aim of the Luftwaffe was to force Britain to surrender with intensive bombing; failing that, to create conditions suitable for a sea-borne invasion by gaining and keeping air superiority over the landing areas. The aim of RAF Fighter Command was to stay in being as a viable force

to defend against invasion, at the same time seeking to defeat the Luftwaffe by inflicting unacceptable levels of attrition.

The initiative lay with the Luftwaffe; all Fighter Command could do was to respond to each threat as best it could. For the British, the saving grace was that the Me 109, the most potent German fighter, had a very limited radius of action, while the long-range escort fighter, the Me 110, had already proved no match for Spitfires and Hurricanes. This meant that the lion's share of the action would be limited to south-eastern England and the south coast. As it happened, the campaign unfolded in four fairly distinct phases.

Even though victorious in France, the Luftwaffe had taken heavy losses. It needed to

Dornier Do 17s over London on September 7 1940. The first day of the all-out assault on the capital caught the defenders on the wrong foot; they expected a continuation of airfield attacks and allowed the bombers to slip through.

be brought up to strength once more, to train new aircrew and to move to new bases in Occupied Europe. All this took time, and at first German resources were scanty.

The opening phase was exploratory; attacks on British convoys in the Channel and Thames Estuary, coupled with fighter sweeps over south-eastern England.

Convoy raids were difficult to counter. Standing patrols, typically consisting of three or six fighters, were prevented from reaching the bombers by superior numbers of German fighters. At best only a few minutes early warning was available, and getting reinforcements airborne in time to intercept often proved impossible. Not until the fighting moved inland and warning times became longer was the RAF control system able to really prove itself.

The fighter sweeps, in Gruppe or even Geschwader strength, proved easier to counter. As fighters could inflict little damage on ground targets, there was no point in intercepting them. To do so would have been to play the German game. If they could be identified in time, they were left strictly alone, to suffer the attrition inevitable in operations from semi-prepared fields.

The second phase of the battle opened in August, when the Luftwaffe commenced a determined attempt to destroy Fighter Command. The opening move was a concerted attack on the radar stations. While considerable damage was caused, various emergency measures concealed its full extent from German monitoring stations, leading them to conclude that radar stations were very difficult targets to knock out. The attacks were not followed up; an error of the first magnitude. Had the Luftwaffe forgotten that their successful interceptions of

RAF bombers in December 1939 had been largely due to radar early warning?

Throughout the first phase, German reconnaissance airplanes had been very active. With plentiful resources, Fighter Command had harassed them, often scrambling several sections of fighters to deal with each lone intruder. To avoid interception, the recce machines flew ever higher, to the stage where definition from their cameras was reduced. They could still tell which British airfields were in use, but not what was using them.

Consequently, when in the second phase heavy attacks were launched against British bases, much of the effort was wasted against airfields of Coastal or Training Commands; targets which were irrelevant to defeating the RAF fighter force.

This phase saw the heaviest fighting of the battle. German losses over the first six days came

Smoke pluming from its damaged starboard engine, a Dornier Do 17Z heads earthwards for the final time. Bombers were the main target for the defending fighters, and sufficient attrition was inflicted on them to force the battle to be called off.

Heinkel He 111Hs in close formation storm in over southern England during the Battle of Britain. They were however tactical rather than strategic bombers, and were to a degree unsuited to the task that they had been set.

to 244, of which 125 were bombers. Nor were RAF fighter losses light; almost 100 were lost in combat during this period.

In some ways, however, the fighting in August was decisive. The Ju 87 Stuka divebombers, which had terrorized ground forces in Poland and France, were decimated by Spitfires and Hurricanes, and withdrawn, while the loss of 63 of the vaunted Me 110s during this period led to their use being restricted. At the same time, the Me 109 units were ordered to provide close escort for the bombers.

This is generally regarded as a tactical error. In combat, fighters seek the advantages of speed, height and initiative. Tied to the bombers in the close escort mission, these are lost. The German fighter pilots, weaving to stay with the bombers, and having to allow the British fighters to attack before they could respond, felt most unhappy about it. Be that as it may, the figures tell another story. Over the next two weeks, average German combat attrition of all types more than

halved, while Me 109 and British fighter losses remained steady at the previous level!

Hard fighting and continued attacks on their bases took an increasing toll on the British fighters, but this was not immediately obvious to the Luftwaffe. Just when the situation of Fighter Command looked desperate, the Germans switched targets. Seeking a decisive fighter battle, they turned their attention to London, transferring almost all fighter units to the Pas-de-Calais for the purpose. At first this appeared to work; the response of Fighter Command was unimpressive, and the capital sustained massive damage. German intelligence calculated that their stubborn enemy was down to its last 50 Spitfires, and that one last effort should clinch matters.

Sunday September 15 saw what was to be the decisive effort. In the morning, London was attacked by a mere 25 Dorniers, escorted by 150 Me 109s. Fighter Command scrambled 23 squadrons, which became embroiled with the

The most advanced Luftwaffe bomber defense measure was this turret mounting a single 12.7mm Rheinmetall-Borsig MG-131 machine gun. It was far inferior to British and American powered turrets.

seen, their fighting formations were basically inferior to those of the Jagdflieger. Having ceded the initiative, they could do little other than respond to the German attacks. How then had they triumphed?

The formal Fighting Area Attacks against bombers had proved useless in the presence of escort fighters. While the ground-controlled interception system allowed fighter squadrons to be scrambled and directed against incoming raids, the elapsed time was generally too short to allow the use of clever tactics. The usual method was to go straight in. With escort fighters around and usually above, there was little time to jockey for position beforehand. This had its advantages; the Germans soon learned that the mere appearance of British fighters was the immediate prelude to a savage attack.

A widely used method was to go in head-on, in wide line abreast or flat echelon, with all guns blazing. To German bomber crews, huddled unprotected in the glazed noses of their airplanes, this was a fearsome sight. Often this first pass split up the bombers, making individual machines vulnerable to a second attack from the traditional astern position.

escorts in a ferocious running battle.

The Dorniers managed to reach the southern suburbs of London, where they were met by 60 fighters in parade-ground order. This was the Duxford Wing, led by the legendary Douglas Bader. The myth of the "last 50 Spitfires" was instantly shattered, with incalculable consequences for the Luftwaffe. From this point on, they knew absolutely that they were not winning.

Two further raids on London resulted in heavy losses for the Luftwaffe, then the daylight assault was terminated. This led to the fourth phase of the battle, attacks by fighter-bombers.

Difficult to intercept, the Jabos caused little damage, while as summer came to an end flying was reduced, and the Battle of Britain quietly drew to a close.

The first air campaign in which ground forces played no part, the Battle of Britain was a landmark in air combat. The defenders were usually outnumbered in the air and, as we have

Over 50 hits are visible in this picture of a damaged bomber, but it survived and returned to base. Rifle-caliber machine guns lacked destructive power. Guns of 0.50in caliber or 20mm cannon would have scored fewer hits, yet had a better chance of destroying this bomber.

Many British squadron commanders had by now realized that the basic three-ship section contained one aircraft too many. Sailor Malan of 74 Squadron devised his own formation, which was adopted by many other units. Instead of two six-ship flights, the squadron was broken down into fours in line astern, each of two pairs: the shooter and his protective wingman or, as the Russians put it, the spear and the shield. While this was still tactically inferior to the German Schwarm, it was a great advance.

Regarded as a fighter versus fighter contest, adjudicated by the number of losses suffered, the Battle of Britain was a German victory, although the margin was small. But on all other counts; total losses, and most important of all, the attainment of the objective, it was a resounding victory for the British.

THE NIGHT AIR WAR

Night fighting had always been the poor relation. In the Great War, the Royal Flying Corps had defeated the lumbering Zeppelins, but had achieved little against bombers. Tactical night raiding over France had been met by fighters following the roads and rivers of Flanders, seeking to spot opponents against the lighter night sky, with little success. To be fair, it must be said that night bombers had great difficulty in locating their targets, and even greater difficulty in hitting them. If the threat was ineffective, little effort was needed to counter it.

As related earlier, RAF Bomber Command had been forced to switch to night raiding at an early stage. During the Battle of Britain, the Luftwaffe followed suit, as the only way in which it could damage British war industry which lay beyond the reach of escort fighters.

Finding the target is essential in night fighting. For this two things are necessary. The first is to know precisely where the target is, where it is going, and how fast. The second is for the night fighter to know precisely where it is in relation to the target. Of the two, the second is probably the most difficult to achieve.

The obvious solution was to capitalize on the human eyeball; to turn night into day by means of searchlights. This involved many problems; firstly the searchlights had to illuminate the bomber. Secondly, the fighter had to be below the bombers in order to see their illuminated undersides. Thirdly, the night fighter had to be near enough to be able to catch the bomber while climbing. Fourthly the sky had to be fairly clear of cloud and haze. The fact that these conditions were rare over Northern Europe meant that this was easier said than done.

Both British and Germans had radar, and while this could indicate the position, course and speed of the bomber, this meant little if the fighter did not know its own position precisely.

BRISTOL BEAUFIGHTER IF

Dimensions: 57ft 10in (17.63m);
Length 41ft 8in (12.70m); Height 15ft 10in (4.83m);
Wing area 503sq.ft (46.73m²).
Power: Two Bristol Hercules IX 14-cylinder air-cooled radial engines rated at 1,500hp each.
Weights: Empty c14,500lb (6,577kg);
Loaded 20,800lb (9,435kg).
Performance: Maximum speed 323mph (520km/hr); Ceiling 28,900ft (8,808m);
Climb 3min 30sec to 5,000ft (1,524m);
Range 1,500 miles (2,414km).
Armament: Four nose-mounted 20mm Hispano cannon with 60 rounds per gun, and six wing-mounted 7.62mm Browning machine guns.

As the first ever effective radar-equipped night fighter, the Beaufighter has assured its place in the hall of fame. Big enough to carry on-board radar, it also had the performance to catch German night raiders during the first years of the war, and armament heavy enough to destroy them with a single short burst. Developed in haste, using wings, fuselage and empennage from the Beaufort torpedo bomber, its handling qualities left much to be desired, and it was laterally unstable. Originally the 20mm cannon were drum-fed, but this was later changed to belt-feeding. Tough and versatile, the Beaufighter served in many other roles.

Junkers Ju 88 night fighter. It was adapted from the bomber variant with the addition of a solid nose and a battery of forward firing guns. This is the early intruder variant without AI radar. Photo left shows the poor forward view from the cockpit.

There were two basic solutions to the problem. The first was airborne radar carried in a fighter with a specialist operator; the second was the intruder mission, carried out over enemy bomber bases, where targets could frequently be found as they took off, heavy with fuel and bombs, or landed, tired and careless after a long mission. Few intruder pilots enjoyed much success; German Wilhelm Beier was credited with 14 victories; a Czech Hurricane pilot with the RAF, Karel Kuttelwascher, achieved 15 intruder victories.

The answer was of course airborne radar (AI). The British had gained a considerable lead in this field. A few AI-equipped Blenheims defended England during the early phase of the night war, but the performance of these was inadequate. The first really effective AI-equipped night fighter was the Beaufighter which, despite difficulties in handling, had the speed and rate of climb to catch the bombers,

even when the latter had unloaded and were homeward-bound, and the firepower to knock them down with a short burst.

AI-assisted night fighting called for teamwork. While the pilot flew his airplane, the AI operator was responsible for pointing him in the right direction. Inland radar stations proliferated, and ground control from these, in contact with both bomber and night fighter, was used to place the latter within about 3 miles(5km) of the target.

Developed as a fast light bomber, the Bristol Blenheim was pressed into service as a long range fighter, and then as a night fighter. In the latter role, performance was inadequate against German bombers.

A Heinkel He 111 prepares to take off for a target in England. The night Blitz was at first successful but, as the British defenses were strengthened, losses rose. The pilot of the Heinkel had a raiseable seat which enabled him to land with his head outside the "glass nose".

The De Havilland Mosquito night fighter was, like many others, derived from a light bomber. Whether on the defensive, acting as an intruder, or in the bomber support role, it was equally successful.

From this distance the AI operator could hopefully gain contact, and from indications on two, or in the early German case three, cathode ray tubes, he had to deduce not only where the target was, but what it was doing. Early AI radar sets suffered from squint, which led them to produce false indications. This made the task of the operator even more difficult.

The problem was then to guide his pilot to within visual distance of the target, from where it could be identified as hostile. Even on the darkest night, the sky was always slightly lighter than the ground, with the horizon the lightest area of all. The trick was to approach from slightly low to illuminate the target against the sky, while concealing the night fighter against the darker ground.

Visual distance varied according to conditions. On a bright moonlit night, an airplane might be spotted at a mile or more; on a really dark night this reduced to 300ft(90m) or less, and even then was no more than a two-dimensional silhouette. One of the problems with radar was that, as well as a maximum range, it also had a minimum range. Under adverse conditions this was less than visual range, which caused difficulties.

NIGHT FIGHTER PERFORMANCE
1939-42

Type	Origin	Max Speed mph(km/hr)	Rate of Climb	Ceiling(ft/m)
Blenheim	Britain	266/428	15min to 15,000ft/4,572m	22,000/6,705
Me 110G-4	Germany	297/478	c11min to 18,046ft/5,500m	26,248/8,000
Ju 88C-6	Germany	307/494	26min 24sec to 30,185ft/9,200m	32,480/9,900
Mosquito	Britain	378/608	7min 30sec to 15,000ft/4,572m	36,000/10,972

The Boston BD 7 was adapted as a night fighter and intruder by the RAF as the Havoc. One variant was equipped with radar and a search-light, and accompanied by two Hurricanes, but this was a failure.

When the contact slipped from the screens, the night fighter crew knew that something was out there, very close, but still invisible. Too high an overtaking speed would probably result in a midair collision; too low might allow the target to escape. Only a gifted radar operator could direct his pilot in astern at just the right speed to make visual contact.

The learning process was slow, but it was steady. In January 1941, RAF night fighters flew 486 sorties, gained 78 contacts, but made only three claims. Five months later sorties quadrupled, but claims rose to 96. German losses in this period went from 0.02 per cent to 3.93 per cent; a factor of nearly 200! Only the movement to the Russian Front in May 1941 prevented further increases. The cover of darkness was no longer absolute, and the night fighter, if not yet actually master of the situation, had showed its potential.

Meanwhile British bombers roved the length and breadth of the Third Reich, giving German night fighters the same problems as their RAF counterparts had already overcome. They had however two advantages. Deep over the continent, the weather was less variable than it was over Britain, while the distances flown by British bombers were much greater than those of the Germans, putting them at risk for longer, giving the German night fighters more time to react.

Although in some fields German radar research was ahead of the British, this was not the case with AI. At first they relied on ground control bringing the night fighter into visual range of its target, but it was soon realized that this was insufficient. After a brief flirtation with infra-red, they turned to AI radar.

Like the RAF, they had no purpose-designed night fighters, and were forced to adapt what was available. Having been less than successful as a day fighter, the Me 110 was an obvious choice. AI radar was crammed in, as was a third seat for the operator. The others were modified bombers; Dornier Do 17Zs and 215s, and Junkers Ju 88Cs.

The first German AI-assisted night victory took place on August 9 1941. As with the British, early progress was hampered by unreliability, and only gradually was the new equipment accepted. But when it was, British bomber losses started to rise.

LEANING FORWARD

By the spring of 1941, with the danger of invasion removed, RAF Fighter Command adopted a more aggressive policy. Whereas in the previous summer they had fought a defensive battle, they now sought to carry the fight to the enemy. Rhubarbs and Rangers were incursions of small numbers of fighters, typically a pair, looking for targets of opportunity. Rodeos were fighter sweeps, typically anything up to six squadrons of 72 airplanes, but like the Jagdflieger sweeps of a year earlier, these often failed to entice the enemy fighters to battle.

Most used was the Circus, a handful of bombers as bait, protected by a hundred or more fighters. The basic RAF Fighter Command unit of this period was the wing, typically consisting of three squadrons of Spitfires. This had given rise to a new command: the Wing Leader. The first two Wing Leaders were Sailor Malan at Biggin Hill, and Douglas Bader at Tangmere.

Bader, the man with two artificial legs, was arguably the most inspirational fighter leader of all time. It was during this period that he introduced his version of the German Schwarm, the finger-four, so called because the position of the airplanes resembled the fingertips of an outstretched hand. Once adopted, this system lasted well beyond the end of the war.

As a fighter, the Hurricane had now reached the end of its development potential, although the IIC, with a more powerful engine and four 20mm cannon made it still an opponent to be reckoned with. By contrast, the Spitfire still had a long way to go. Given a more powerful Merlin engine rated at 1,440hp, and armed with two 20mm Hispano cannon and four Browning machine guns, it became the Mark VB.

Nor did German fighter development stand

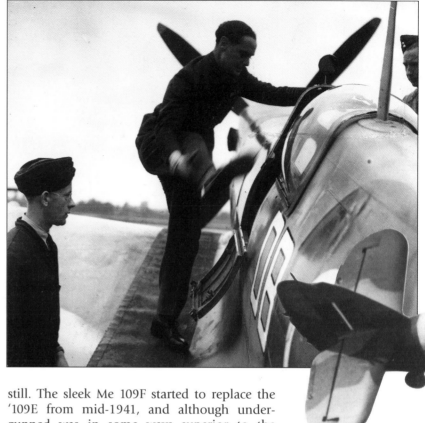

still. The sleek Me 109F started to replace the '109E from mid-1941, and although under-gunned was in some ways superior to the Spitfire VB. Not long after, it was supplanted by the Me 109G which, although more potent, had some rather nasty handling qualities.

In more than two years of war, RAF fighter pilots had become accustomed to being able to outmaneuver their opponents, forcing the Jagdflieger to fight a hit and run battle. A frequent complaint of this period was: "Why doesn't Jerry stay and fight?"

The combat debut of the Focke Wulf FW 190A in the fall of 1941 came as a terrible shock. The Spitfire V was outclassed, not only in climb and

FOCKE-WULF FW 190A-3

Dimensions: Span 34ft 5½in (10.50m); Length 29ft 0in (8.84m); Height 13ft 0in (3.96m); Wing area 197sq.ft (18.30m²).
Power: One BMW 801Dg 14-cylinder air-cooled radial rated at 1,700hp.
Weights: Empty 6,020lb (2,731kg); Loaded 8,770lb (3,978kg).
Performance: Maximum speed 399mph (642km/hr); Ceiling 33,794ft (10,300m); Climb 9min 54sec to 20,014ft (6,100m); Range 644 miles (1,036km).
Armament: Two nose-mounted 7.9mm MG 17 machine guns; two 20mm Mauser MG 151 cannon in the wing roots, and two wing-mounted 20mm Oerlikon MGFF cannon.

If the Me 109 was a thoroughbred, the FW 190A was designed as a cavalry horse; rugged and capable, with tremendous firepower. The new Mauser MG 151 cannon were much faster firing, had greater muzzle velocity, and a heavier projectile than the MGFFs outboard. After

becoming operational late in 1941, it soon showed that it out-performed the Spitfire V in all departments except turn radius. Roll rate was exceptionally fast, which enabled the German fighter to change direction very quickly, although it was unforgiving if pushed too hard: an irrecoverable high speed stall and spin was the usual result.

Left: Douglas Bader, arguably the most inspirational fighter leader of the war, lifts one of his artificial legs into the cockpit of his Spitfire. More than any other leader, he was responsible for getting RAF fighter tactics right.

RAF fighter guns went from one extreme to the other. The Hurricane I, with eight .303in (7.7mm) machine guns, was adapted to carry four 20mm Hispano cannon, giving it the greatest firepower of any fighter during the early war period.

dive, but in rate of roll. While the new German fighter could not match the turn rate of the Spitfire, it could negate this advantage by rolling into the turn much faster. Now "Jerry" stayed and fought as never before, and the Spitfire V pilots were the losers by it.

New and better Spitfires were under development, but Fighter Command could not afford to wait for them. A stop-gap was rushed into service; the Spitfire IX. This was basically a Spitfire V with a Merlin engine rated at 1,710hp, with a two-speed, two-stage supercharger. Performance was very similar to that of the FW 190A-3, although the German fighter was still faster in rate of roll and the dive. Only at very high altitudes, where the FW 190A was rarely found, did the Spitfire IX hold an overall superiority.

The "leaning forward into France" policy was in many ways a failure. British losses generally exceeded those of the Luftwaffe, although overclaiming, the perennial bugbear of air historians, served to obscure the fact. Its only real success was to keep the air weapon sharp through usage.

This failure was highlighted by the Dieppe raid in August 1942. British and American forces put up no fewer than 2,462 fighter sorties over the beachhead, losing 114 airplanes in the process. German losses amounted to 48, of which only 20 were fighters. The lesson of Dieppe was that air umbrellas leak.

Towards the end of 1942, the Circus fell into disuse. Low-level penetrations by light and medium bombers were far more damaging than the "bait" originally used, while the USAAF had started to raid occupied Europe. Escorting the American heavies became far more important than trying to bring the Luftwaffe to battle.

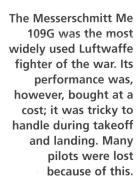

The Messerschmitt Me 109G was the most widely used Luftwaffe fighter of the war. Its performance was, however, bought at a cost; it was tricky to handle during takeoff and landing. Many pilots were lost because of this.

Sun and Sand

1940-1943

WHEN ITALY ENTERED the war on June 10 1940, the situation of the British in the Middle East looked distinctly unpromising. Prewar rearmament had naturally concentrated on the needs of home defense, and the outposts of Empire had to make shift with the left-overs. The island of Malta, strategically placed across the Italian supply routes between Sicily and Libya, had no fighter defense at all. Four crated Sea Gladiators were hurriedly assembled, to be flown by volunteers, most of them flying boat pilots with little or no fighter experience. Egypt was slightly better defended, with three squadrons of Gladiators and a handful of ancient Gauntlets.

Against them was ranged the might of the Regia Aeronautica. Numerically strong, it contained nearly 2,000 combat aircraft, with a similar number available as an attrition reserve. They were however widely spread between Italy itself, Sicily and Sardinia, Libya, Rhodes, and Albania, which had been annexed during the previous year. Almost 200 were based in Ethiopia and Somalia, although as these were cut off from

the homeland they were of little value.

The Regia Aeronautica had been built up in the early and mid-1930s, and by 1940 many of its airplanes were obsolescent. Re-equipment with more modern machines was under way, but the process was slow. While Italian airplane design was excellent, engine development had not kept pace. To compensate for this lack, adequate bomber performance could only be attained by using three engines.

While this gave Italian bombers an antiquated appearance, they were in fact quite efficient. The best of them, the Savoia-Marchetti S.79 Sparviero, cruised quite happily at 221mph (355km/hr). This made it difficult for a Gladiator to intercept unless it was well placed at the outset, while at full throttle the Italian bomber could outpace the British fighter at most altitudes.

The cult of the fighter ace had not caught the Italian imagination to the same degree as it had with other nations, with the result that fighter development had become comparatively neglected. At the outbreak of war, most Italian fighter units were still equipped with biplanes: elderly Fiat CR.32s, and the rather more modern CR.42 Falco. The latter, although of rather better performance than the Gladiator, was barely fast enough to escort the S.79.

A few monoplane fighters were entering service, notably the Fiat G.50 Freccia and Macchi C.200 Saetta. Like the bombers, these also suffered from the lack of a high-powered fighter engine, and were fitted with the Fiat A.74 RC 38 14-cylinder radial developing 870hp. Performance was also reduced by a hang-up from Spanish Civil War experience. There, the nimble CR.32s had been forced to rely on agility to counter the better-performing Republican I-16s. Consequently maneuver combat, the time-honored dogfight, had become all important in Italian minds.

The pilot had to be given two things: the best

The early months of the war in the Middle East were spearheaded by the Gloster Gladiator. Not fast enough to intercept the Italian bombers, the Gladiator did perform well against Italian CR.32 and CR.42 biplane fighters.

possible forward view, and the ability to take deflection shots without the target becoming obscured below the nose. This was done by placing the pilot's seat high up in the fuselage, producing a hump-backed silhouette, and reducing aerodynamic cleanliness, with predictably adverse effects on performance.

Nor had Italian fighter pilots benefited from their Spanish Civil War experiences. Reliance on maneuvrability had to a degree obscured the need to develop proper tactics and teamwork. In general the Italians were splendid aerobatic pilots, but failed to realize that standard aerobatics such as rolls and loops were air display showpieces, with little or no relevance to combat. Thus equipped and trained, the Regia Aeronautica went to war.

The air war in the Middle East took place over vast areas and lasted for three years. Discounting the skirmishing in East Africa, it encompassed four major theaters, all of which impinged upon each other to a greater or lesser extent, and which drew in other major players. Before examining each theater in turn, it is necessary to take an overview.

At the outbreak of war, the RAF in Egypt, disregarding its numerical inferiority, immediately took the offensive, with fighter

patrols, raids and reconnaissances into Libya. The Italians retaliated in kind. The inadequacies of the opposing fighter forces were now exposed; RAF Gladiators were hard pressed to catch the Italian Sparvieros, while Fiat CR.42s were barely able, and CR.32s were completely unable, to catch British Blenheims. But when the opposing biplane fighters met, some fierce battles took place. Gradually a trickle of Hurricanes reached Egypt, and in August the

In the desert war long range was at a premium. Although out-classed by most Axis fighters the Beaufighter played an exemplary part in interdicting Axis supplies, and was very successful against transport aircraft.

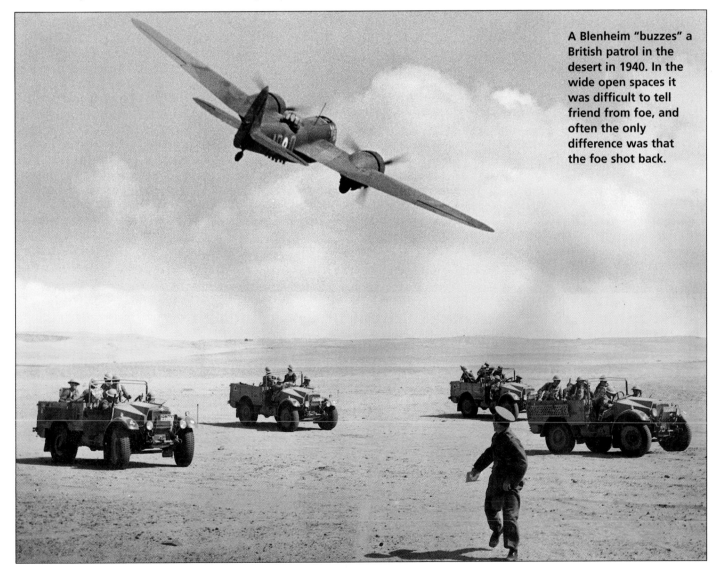

A Blenheim "buzzes" a British patrol in the desert in 1940. In the wide open spaces it was difficult to tell friend from foe, and often the only difference was that the foe shot back.

HAWKER HURRICANE IIC

Dimensions: Span 40ft (12.19m);
Length 32ft 3in (9.83m); Height 13ft 1½in (4m);
Wing area 257½sq.ft (23.92m²).
Power: One Rolls-Royce Merlin liquid-cooled V-12
rated at 1,280hp.
Weights: Empty 5,800lb (2,631kg);
Loaded 7,800lb (3,538kg).
Performance: Maximum speed 339mph (545km/hr);
Ceiling 35,600ft (10,850m); Climb 9min 6sec to 20,000ft
(6,096m); Range 460 miles (740km).
Armament: Four wing-mounted 20mm Hispano cannon.

While the Hurricane I earned its laurels over France and in the Battle of Britain, its inferior performance made it more easily spared than the Spitfire for other theaters of war. In addition to night fighting, it became the foremost defender of Malta in 1941; and the primary British fighter in the early desert war and the ill-fated Greek venture. It also served with distinction in Burma and the Far East. Although slower than the Kittyhawk, it out-performed the American fighter in all other departments; was far more maneuvrable, while the Hurricane IIC armament of four 20mm cannon gave unprecedented hitting power.

first Hurricane squadron was formed. From this moment, Italian bomber losses rose, while their fighters were outclassed.

The Italian ground offensive started in September, but was quickly halted. Then on December 9 the British moved forward in what was intended to be little more than a large-scale raid, supported by aggressive air action, with fighters strafing. The result was astonishing; the Italian front virtually collapsed in a matter of days. Soon the road to Tripoli, and complete victory, lay open, only to be squandered on another venture.

On October 28, Italy, operating from Albania, invaded Greece. Three squadrons of Blenheim

Desert conditions were always difficult. Here we see a Fordson tracked vehicle towing a Hurricane. Once the war of movement started, most things had to be done by hand, as the various facilities had been left far behind.

bombers and two of Gladiator fighters were sent to assist the Greeks. Fierce fighting followed over the next few months; more reinforcements were thrown in, but then the Germans intervened once again, overrunning the Balkans in a matter of weeks.

Weakened by the need to reinforce Greece, the British army heading for Tripoli was halted. This was disastrous. Concerned at the continued failures of his ally, Hitler determined to keep Italy in the war. He despatched two German mechanized divisions to Libya, commanded by the soon to be famous Erwin Rommel. A brilliant series of counterstrokes followed, and by April, the weakened British forces were back in Egypt. The Germans, backed by Luftwaffe units, were in the desert to stay.

This was not the first German intervention on behalf of Italy. Malta, the unsinkable aircraft carrier ideally placed to interdict supply convoys between Italy and Libya, had proved a thorn in the side of the Axis from the outset. Italian attempts to bomb the island into submission had failed woefully.

The original handful of Sea Gladiators had been replaced by Hurricanes, forcing the Regia Aeronautica to provide fighter escorts. Early in 1941, a single Staffel of Me 109Es arrived on Sicily. The Hurricanes were outclassed, and before long Malta had been neutralized as an offensive base.

The essential in the desert was keeping sand out of the engine, for which filters were needed. Here we see Me 109E-7/Trop fighters adapted for desert conditions.

This did not last. Luftwaffe units were withdrawn from all fronts to take part in the invasion of Russia in June 1941, and Malta recovered. With Rommel's German army at risk in North Africa, this could not be allowed, and the Luftwaffe returned in force later that year. The first half of 1942 saw a concerted attempt to bomb Malta out of the war, but this was foiled by the arrival of large numbers of Spitfires.

Meanwhile the war in the desert had rolled back and forth as first one side, then the other, overstretched their lines of supply. But all the time Allied strength was growing, and with tremendous air support the decisive Battle of El Alamein in October/November 1942 rolled back the Axis forces for the final time.

Even as this took place, an Anglo-American force landed in the north-west of the continent. The final air battles of the North African campaign took place over Tunisia in the late spring of 1943.

THE WESTERN DESERT

There was no comparison between the early warning system in Egypt and that in England. At first there were only three radar stations, supplemented later by a few inadequate mobile sets, and these were insufficient to allow tracking. Fighter control, as at the Battle of Britain, simply did not exist. Inland was a network of observer posts, but far more widely scattered than those in England, with observers reporting by unreliable wireless telegraphy. The main difference was the usually cloudless skies of the Middle East, which aided visual tracking. The most valuable detection aid of all was the Y-service, which monitored enemy radio transmissions. Rudimentary at first, it was brought to a fine pitch of efficiency, which continued throughout the entire three years of the desert campaign,

As the Italians had no radar, and no observation network to speak of, most combats in the early months were the result of chance

The Desert Air Force employed fighters which were generally inferior to the Me 109 until the arrival of the Spitfire V in 1942. This machine is a Spitfire VB of 601 Squadron.

encounters. Ports were among the few strategic targets available. For the rest, there were hardly any rail links, or even proper roads, let alone bridges which could be cut. Barracks and supply dumps were valuable targets, but the over-riding need was for air superiority. Gladiators patrolled near the frontier at dawn and dusk, but rarely encountered enemy aircraft, bombers or fighter escorts.

Air superiority is not always best achieved in the air. Ever mindful of the fact that airplanes are at their most vulnerable on the ground, Blenheim light bombers of 45 Squadron were sent to raid the Italian airfield at El Adem shortly after dawn on June 11. Achieving complete surprise, they burned two hangars and destroyed several airplanes. This was a promising start. More raids followed, and the Italians started to mount regular patrols in their turn. Clashes between opposing aircraft gradually became more frequent.

On July 4 six Gladiators escorting a Lysander spotted nine CR.42s of 2° Stormo taking off from Monastir. Diving to the attack, they caught the Fiats before they could get either altitude or flying speed. In the ensuing mêlée, several CR.42s were shot down and others damaged. In this and one other combat on the day, this Italian unit lost six, with another four badly damaged. All but one of the Gladiators returned safely.

On the whole, the British fighters had rather the better of the tactical skirmishing of this early period, but intercepting fast Sparviero bombers attempting to bomb warships in Alexandria harbour from high altitude proved virtually impossible without adequate early warning. Even Pat Pattle, the top-scoring Allied fighter ace of the war, and top-scoring Gladiator pilot with 15 victories, managed to account for only one S.79, and that was over Greece, where conditions were slightly more favorable.

With the opening of the trans-Africa ferry route, sufficient Hurricanes arrived to allow a flight to be formed in 80 Squadron. Life for the high-level Italian raiders at once became much more uncertain. On August 17, John Lapsley, flying a lone Hurricane, intercepted three S.79s near Bardia and shot them all down. A few days later, 274 Squadron was formed in Egypt, equipped entirely with Hurricanes, including all those previously with 80 Squadron.

In June, much of the Italian force in Libya had been deployed on the Tunisian border, facing the French. When the latter capitulated, much of

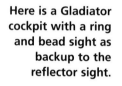

Here is a Gladiator cockpit with a ring and bead sight as backup to the reflector sight.

Gladiators return to base in the Western Desert, often described as "miles and miles of sweet Fanny Adams".

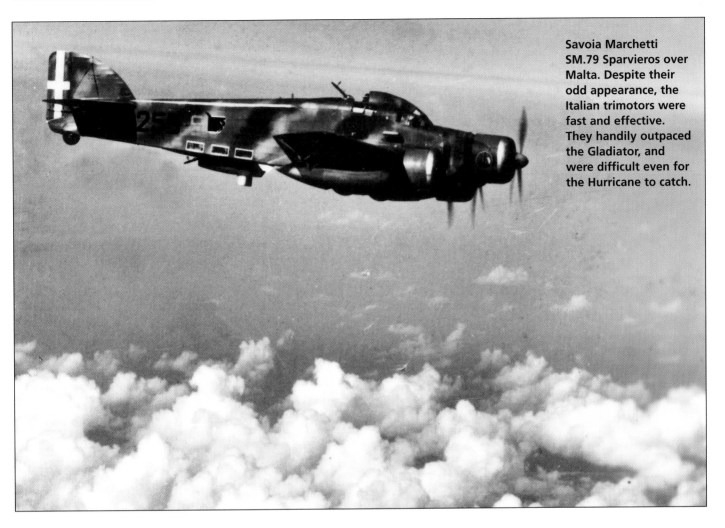

Savoia Marchetti SM.79 Sparvieros over Malta. Despite their odd appearance, the Italian trimotors were fast and effective. They handily outpaced the Gladiator, and were difficult even for the Hurricane to catch.

it, including most of the Regia Aeronautica units, was transferred eastwards towards the Egyptian frontier. By the end of July this was substantially complete, but the Italians were in no hurry.

Meanwhile the Italian fighters concentrated on flying standing patrols to protect the build-up on the ground, and also the supply ports. British reconnaissance continued, with fighter escort, but these flights often encountered superior numbers. On one such occasion, three out of four Gladiators were lost, and the pilot of the fourth was wounded.

Not until September 13 did the Italians cross the frontier into Egypt, and when they did they ground to a halt well before reaching the forward British positions. There they stayed for eight weeks, while Allied air power was reinforced. 3 Squadron of the Royal Australian Air Force joined what was to become the Desert Air Force (DAF); the first of many Commonwealth units, including South African squadrons.

With little action on the ground, three light bomber and two Gladiator squadrons were sent to help the Greeks hold off the Italian invasion launched from Albania. Even with this reduction in strength, the DAF maintained the ascendancy, and when on December 9 a limited British offensive was launched, it was greatly helped by the aggressive use of air power.

Constantly the DAF patrolled and strafed Italian airfields, destroying the Regia Aeronautica in the air and on the ground. The fortunes of war were not always one-sided; on December 12 five Gladiators of 3 RAAF Squadron were shot down by CR.42s, for a solitary victory. But by now several units had been equipped with Hurricanes, which completely outclassed the Falcos as long as no attempt was made to turn with them.

On December 18, 20° Gruppo, equipped with Fiat G.50bis Freccias, arrived in the desert. Handily out-performed in all departments even by the Hurricane I, and comparatively undergunned, this made little impact on the fighting. Even against the Gladiator, the G.50 achieved little; some 25 per cent of Gladiator victories were scored against the Freccia. This was of course mainly due to Italian pilots

The Fiat G.50bis Freccia was the first Italian monoplane fighter to enter service. Less maneuvrable than the Gladiator and undergunned, its impact on the air war was minimal.

The Macchi C.200 Saetta was exceptionally maneuvrable. Similar in appearance to the G.50, it was a far superior fighter, and could out- turn, outclimb and out- dive the Hurricane. It was however slower than the British fighter in level flight.

trying to dogfight with the far more maneuvrable biplane.

The British ground offensive succeeded beyond everyone's wildest dreams and, continually harassed from the air, the Italian army was soon in full flight. Italian forward airfields were quickly over-run, and the Regia Aeronautica fell back in disorder. While they had lost only 58 aircraft in action, nearly 1,200 had been captured, although many of the latter were in advanced states of disrepair. The nomadic phase of the desert air war had begun.

To be fully effective, an air force needs fixed bases, with supplies of fuel, munitions, spares and servicing facilities readily available. Operating from temporary airstrips with meagre facilities was a totally different matter. Neither the British nor the Italians were more than marginally prepared for this, and both suffered in consequence.

As the Allied army advanced towards Tobruk, more squadrons were sent to Greece. Then with little between the Allies and Tripoli, and ultimate victory in sight, the army was halted on February 12 1941 in order to provide reinforcements for the Greek venture, leaving only a holding force in Libya.

The next 30 months in the desert saw a continual ebb and flow of battle; first one side and then the other gained the advantage. With Hitler determined to tie Allied forces down by keeping Italy in the war, German reinforcements arrived in the Western Desert. The first German fighter unit to arrive was I/JG 27, in April 1941. Although heavily outnumbered, it was tasked with wresting air superiority from the Allies with Me 109s.

This was more difficult than might have been expected. The first P-40 Tomahawks arrived in June 1941 and, after a short period in which the bugs attendant on the service entry of any new type were eliminated, commenced operations. Although the Me 109E was superior to both the Tomahawk and the Hurricane at altitude, most fighting took place at medium and low levels, where the difference was less marked. On the other hand, the Jagdflieger usually held a positional advantage. But whereas close air support for the Axis forces was supplied by the Ju 87 divebomber, the Allies, with no equivalent, were forced to use fighterbombers. Caught from above while laden with bombs, the Hurricanes and Tomahawks were at an immediate disadvantage once combat was joined.

Another fighter entered the desert war in July 1941. The Macchi C.200 Saetta resembled the G.50 in appearance, but was vastly superior to

MACCHI C.202 FOLGORE

Dimensions: Span 34ft 8½in (10.58m); Length 29ft ½in (8.85m); Height 9ft 11½in (3.04m); Wing area 180.83sq.ft (16.80m²).
Power: One Alfa-Romeo RA 1000 RC 41 Monsoni liquid-cooled V-12 engine rated at 1,400hp.
Weights: Empty 5,185lb (2,352kg); Loaded 6,459lb (2,930kg).
Performance: Maximum speed 370mph (595km/hr); Ceiling 37,730ft (11,500m); Climb 4min 4sec to 16,405ft (5,000m); Range 475 miles (764km).
Armament: Two nose-mounted 12.7mm Breda-SAFAT machine guns with 400 rpg, and two wing-mounted 7.7mm Breda-SAFAT machine guns with 500 rpg.

Just as the happy marriage of the Merlin engine with the Mustang airframe produced one of the outstanding fighters of the war, so too did a Macchi airframe with the German Daimler-Benz DB 601 engine, license-built by Alfa-Romeo. Early Italian engines lacked power, and while their fighters were maneuvrable, performance was inferior. This was corrected with the Monsoni-powered

Folgore, which even Spitfire pilots treated with a great deal of respect. First flown on August 10 1940, the Folgore was an instant success. Handling was a delight, maneuvrability was outstanding, and it entered service in November 1941. Its only fault was lack of firepower, rectified in some models by Mauser MG 151 wing-mounted cannon.

CURTISS P-40 KITTYHAWK III

Dimensions: Span 37ft 4in (11.38m);
Length 31ft 2in (9.47m); Height 10ft 7in (3.22m);
Wing area 236sq.ft (21.92m^2).
Power: One Allison V-1710-81 liquid-cooled engine
rated at 1,700hp.
Weights: Empty 6,400lb (2,903kg);
Loaded 8,500lb (3,856kg).
Performance: Maximum speed 362mph (582km/hr);
Ceiling 30,000ft (9,144m); Climb 9min to 15,000ft
(4,572m); Range 700 miles (1,126km).
Armament: Six wing-mounted 12.7mm Browning
machine guns.

The most modern American fighter of its day, several
hundred P-40s were acquired by the RAF as the
Tomahawk. As performance fell away rapidly over
15,000ft(4,572m) it was unsuitable for fighter
operations over Western Europe, and was used for
low-level tactical reconnaissance. Many were shipped
to North Africa, where close air support was the order
of the day, and high altitude performance was of less
importance. The Tomahawk was replaced by the more
powerful Kittyhawk from early in 1942. Although
generally outclassed by the Me 109, it gave sterling
service as a fighter-bomber in North Africa and Italy, and held the ring for the USAAF against the Japanese in the Pacific in the early years.

it. Exceptionally maneuvrable for a monoplane,
its handling was finger-light, and although
slightly slower than the Hurricane it outclimbed and out-dived the British fighter with
ease. Its combat debut had been delayed by two
unexplained crashes, which caused it to be
grounded for a while, but these were finally
found to be the result of a high-speed stall
caused by a rare combination of circumstances.
Cured by a modification to the wing, the Saetta
proved to be a formidable opponent, although
under-gunned.

The ebb and flow of battle up and down
hundreds of miles of desert had one inevitable
consequence. Fighter operations took place
from advanced and semi-prepared airfields.
Almost any flat stretch of hard surface would
suffice. Serviceability in these conditions
suffered, while constant and often very rapid
moves did nothing to help combat efficiency.
Supplies of fuel, spares and munitions were
often stretched to the limit. Allied and German

air forces both had mobile radar sets, but the
vagaries of desert operations meant that the Y-
service usually gave the best results.

The end of 1941 saw two more fighter types
enter service in the desert. The Kittyhawk was a
more powerful and rather faster variant of the
Tomahawk, although like its predecessor it was
tricky to land. The approved method was to

The feared Stuka; the Junkers Ju 87B dive bomber was widely used against Malta and in North Africa, where its accuracy of bombing was put to good use. In the background is its usual escort, the Me 109.

DAY FIGHTER COMPARISONS, MIDDLE EAST, 1940-1943

Type	Speed (mph/km-hr)	Ceiling (ft/m)	Climb	Range(ml/km)
Gloster Gladiator	246/396	32,900/10,027	9min 42sec to 20,000ft (6,096m).	410/660
Fiat CR.42 Falco	257/413	33,466/10,200	7min to 19,686ft (6,000m)	485/780
Fiat G.50 Freccia	294/473	25,270/7,700	3min 10sec to 9,845ft (3,000m)	621/1000
Macchi C.200 Saetta	313/529	29,200/8,900	5min 52sec to 16,405ft (5,000m).	354/570
Curtiss Tomahawk	345/555	29,500/8,991	2,650ft/min (13.46m/sec).	730/1,175

The Gladiator and the CR.42 were the last of the fighting biplanes.

If one had to force-land, the desert, with its hard surface and unobstructed level areas, was a good place to do it. This Spitfire VB of 92 Squadron has suffered minimal damage and can be recovered for repair.

wheel it in; three-pointers were a recipe for disaster. The other was the Macchi C.202 Folgore. Based on the C.200, but with a license-built Daimler-Benz engine and extremely sleek lines, it was faster and more agile than any Allied fighter in the theater at that time, climbed like a bird and handled like a dream. In many ways it was far superior to the German Me 109F. In fact, much later in the war, when Italy had joined the Allies, the Folgore was often used to escort Spitfire fighter-bombers!

Whilst fighter quality can influence the outcome of combat, the supreme arbiter is pilot quality. This is generally judged on victories claimed. On the Italian side, this is difficult, inasmuch as keeping scores was not officially countenanced. It is however known that Teresio Martinoli claimed 22 victories over the desert and Malta, while Franco Lucchini and Leonardo Ferrulli both claimed 21. At least a dozen others claimed 15 or more.

The top Hurricane ace in the desert was Hamish Dodds of 274 Squadron. His score of 14 destroyed includes six Me 109s and four

C.202s. In addition he claimed six probables and seven damaged, all between December 1941 and June 1942.

Killer Caldwell of 250 Squadron led the Tomahawk pilots with 16 destroyed, half of which were Me 109s, between June and December 1941. In the same period he accounted for two shared destroyed, five probables, and 11 damaged; not bad for someone flying an air inferiority fighter. Caldwell's record is particularly distinguished when one takes into account that three high-scoring German Experten – Wolfgang Lippert, Erbo Graf von Kageneck, and Fifi Stahlschmidt – were among his victims. His final score for the war was 27 and three shared destroyed. Of these three and one shared were scored in the desert while commanding 112 squadron with Kittyhawks, and eight Japanese aircraft while flying Spitfire Vs in the Pacific.

The leading exponent of the Kittyhawk was Billy Drake, also of 112 Squadron, with 13 destroyed between June and December 1942. Five of these were Me 109s, and two were

THE DEFENSIVE CIRCLE

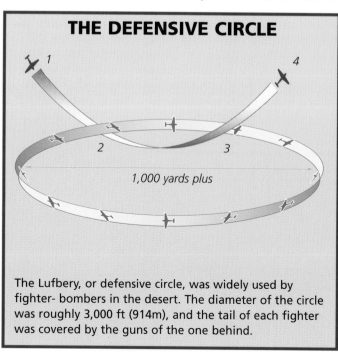

1,000 yards plus

The Lufbery, or defensive circle, was widely used by fighter-bombers in the desert. The diameter of the circle was roughly 3,000 ft (914m), and the tail of each fighter was covered by the guns of the one behind.

AGAINST THE DEFENSIVE CIRCLE

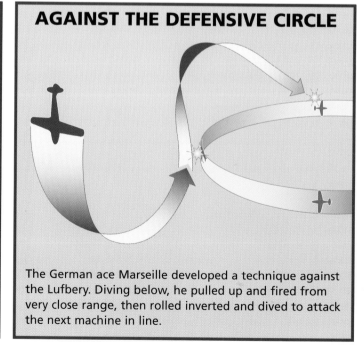

The German ace Marseille developed a technique against the Lufbery. Diving below, he pulled up and fired from very close range, then rolled inverted and dived to attack the next machine in line.

The Me 109 was not used exclusively for air combat, although this was its main role. Here an Me 109E-7/Trop is loaded with a bomb. This was not a great success; the 109 was too delicate for such rough useage.

C.202s. A veteran of the French campaign, his score for the war was 18 destroyed and two shared. Drake was closely followed by Canadian Eddie Edwards of 94 and 260 Squadrons with 13, all single-engined fighters, including high-scoring German Experte Otto Schulz.

These scores are small beer compared with those credited to the Jadgflieger. Jochen Marseille of I/JG 27 was credited with 151 victories in the desert, including 101 P-40s, 30 Hurricanes and 16 Spitfires. While not all of these can be confirmed from the records, his actual score was certainly very high. His success was the result of outstanding aircraft handling, superior tactics, and marksmanship of a high order.

The secret was incredibly precise timing, coupled with inept Allied fighter tactics. Fighter-bombers when intercepted tended to go into a defensive circle in which each was covered by the guns of the fighter astern. The average fighter pilot found this hard to crack, but Marseille was able to dive from outside the circle, pull up from below, then fire from less than 150ft (46m) before pulling away high using the speed of his dive. He fired only when the target dropped from sight beneath his nose, which gave the correct deflection angle!

Marseille's marksmanship was exceptional, and the records show that at the height of his powers he expended an average of 15 shells and bullets per victory. He had his imitators, of which the most successful was Werner Schroer, but none equalled the master. On the other hand it is fair to say that the Allies were unlucky to be bothered by Marseille; seven victories in the Battle of Britain had cost him four airplanes, and within days of his arrival in the desert he was outfought, badly damaged, and forced to crash-land by James Denis, a short and elderly

(35 year-old) Free French Hurricane pilot of 73 Squadron. Denis survived the war with a score of eight destroyed and one shared.

The second highest scorer in North Africa was Werner Schroer with 61 victories out of his eventual total of 114. Having adopted Marseille's dive and shoot methods, Schroer actually bettered Marseille in strike rate, with 1.73 sorties per victory, compared with Marseille's 2.42 sorties per victory.

THE GREEK ADVENTURE

Air combat over Greece was a far cry from the Western Desert. Mountains, which often funnelled airplanes into the valleys, coupled with atrocious weather, with rain and snow which often made the small and muddy Greek airfields inoperable, were a world away from the vast open spaces and clear skies of North Africa.

The wreckage of a Lockheed P-38 Lightning burns in Tunisia as Axis troops look on. They are apparently unconcerned by the possibility of an explosion. The P-38 often fought at medium and low altitudes, where it was not at its best.

Right: Malta saw some of the most intensive air fighting of the war. An unidentified RAF pilot watches approvingly as the thousandth Axis victim is attributed to his Spitfire. The six kill markings look very new against the scruffy paint scheme.

Right: Malta saw some of the most intensive air fighting of the war. An unidentified RAF pilot watches approvingly as the thousandth Axis victim is attributed to his Spitfire. The six kill markings look very new against the scruffy paint scheme.

A sunken gunboat rests on the bottom in Salamis harbor, Greece. British air power had wrested control of the skies from the Italians, but then the Luftwaffe joined the fray in overwhelming strength.

Supplies over the inadequate road systems were a problem, and in the absence of petrol bowsers refueling was done by hand from drums; a time-consuming process.

The tasks of the British Gladiator squadrons were twofold: intercepting Italian raids and escorting their own Blenheim bombers. Once again, with no early warning system available, encounters were very much a matter of chance. They were opposed by Falcos and Freccias from the outset, and were usually heavily out-numbered, often called upon to oppose formations of 40 or more.

The absence of early warning lent itself to raids against airfields, which were almost impossible to fend off, even though use was made of the wasteful and inefficient system of standing patrols.

Hurricanes arrived in Greece in late February 1941, and after only a day or two familiarizing themselves with the type the British pilots went into action. Over the next five weeks, Pat Pattle,

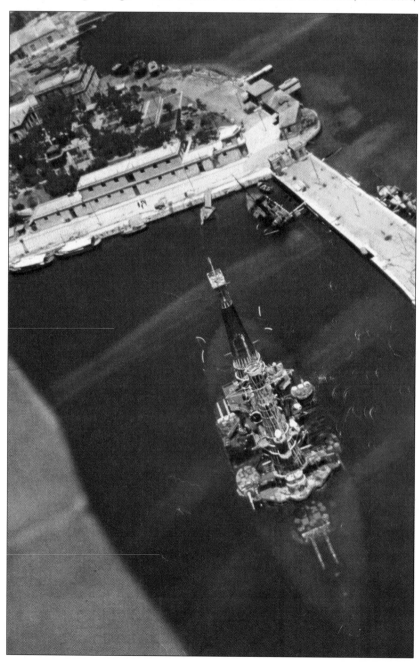

the top-scoring Gladiator ace, added another ten to his tally.

Although initially victorious both on land and in the air, events conspired to make this a losing campaign for the British fighters. Adolf Hitler, preparing to launch his infamous attack on his erstwhile Soviet allies, became alarmed at the prospect of British forces on his flank, while the overthrow of a pro-Nazi government in Yugoslavia spurred him into action. The Luftwaffe was thrown into the fray in the Balkans, through Yugoslavia and through Germany's ally Bulgaria. Bitter fighting took place, but the outnumbered British fighters were gradually driven from the skies. Pattle brought his score to at least 50 during this phase, his victims including nine Me 109s, one piloted by high-scoring German Experte Kurt Übben, who force-landed. Flying whilst ill and exhausted, Pattle was finally brought down and killed over Piraeus by Me 110s on April 20, when he went to the aid of hard-pressed Hurricane pilot Timber Woods.

The other top-scoring ace of the Greek campaign was Cherry Vale. A Gladiator victory over the desert near Trigh Cappuzzo on July 1 1940 was followed by another nine over Greece before converting to the Hurricane. With this airplane he accounted for another 17, mainly bombers, over Greece and Crete by mid-May 1941. In the following month he shot down three Vichy-French airplanes over Syria to bring his total to 30 for the war, plus several damaged.

MALTA

The defense of Malta is one of the great epics of air warfare. Like the desert war, the tide of battle swung back and forth, but this was more due to external influences, notably events in Russia. Located some 60 miles(97km) south of Sicily, it was for most of the war in the rear of the Axis armies in the desert, and directly athwart their sea lanes whence came the bulk of their supplies.

Barely 20 minutes flying time from Axis air bases on Sicily, Malta was extremely vulnerable to air attack. The first Italian air attacks were desultory, in part due to the fact that Sicily-based units were used to raid French targets in Tunisia. Given the weakness of the defenses, this was just as well. After the capitulation, raids became more regular, and these were met by small-scale fighter opposition.

This gradually increased as a few Hurricanes, originally destined for Egypt, were retained to defend the island. After seven weeks, a dozen Hurricanes were flown to the island from the aircraft carrier HMS *Argus*. While these were reinforced at intervals, there were never enough, but fortunately the Regia Aeronautica was not very aggressive at this stage. By the end of 1940,

Italian losses were 23 bombers and 12 fighters. Claims by Italian fighters during this period amounted to 26 destroyed and eight probables, somewhat on the high side. Claims by bomber gunners were considerably higher. By the end of the year, Malta-based Allied bombers and naval units were taking a terrible toll of the Italian supply convoys to North Africa.

Resplendent in desert camouflage two Me 110s patrol off the coast of Sicily in 1942. The Me 110 proved no match for Allied single-seater single-engined fighters in daylight.

A massive lineup of the superb Macchi C.202 Veltro. A German engine allied to an Italian airframe gave rise to an outstanding fighter, the sole weakness of which was that it was undergunned.

"Black men" rearm this Me 109F of JG 54 "Grünherz". The '109F was armed with a single engine-mounted cannon and two wing-mounted machine guns. The Franz totally outclassed the Hurricane over Malta.

The Luftwaffe first appeared on Sicily in January 1941, and during the following month a single Staffel of Me 109Es arrived to reinforce them. Able to gain height at their leisure to achieve a position of advantage, they outfought the defending Hurricanes. When they were withdrawn in late May, they had claimed 41 victories, of which 18 had fallen to Experte Joachim Müncheberg. Not one German pilot was lost during this time.

During June 1941, more than 100 Hurricane IIBs were flown to Malta from aircraft carriers; enough to equip three squadrons. Air superiority over the Regia Aeronautica was re-established, and once more Malta became an offensive base. Even the superb Macchi C.202, which made its combat debut in October, failed to stem the tide, even though it was several weeks before a Hurricane managed to shoot one down.

Once again the Luftwaffe was forced to intervene before Rommel's Afrika Korps was starved of supplies. Units were rushed from the Russian Front, mainly dive bombers, protected by JG 53 and II/JG 3; about 120 Me 109Fs in all. These, backed by an increasing number of Folgores, heavily outnumbered the defenders.

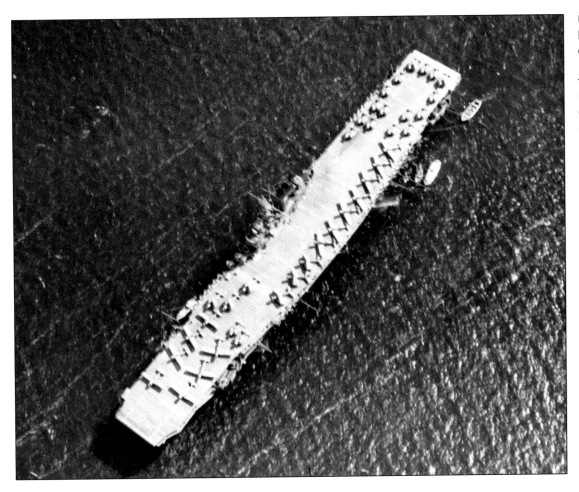

USS *Wasp* was twice loaned to the British during the summer of 1942 to ferry Spitfires to Malta, and this made all the difference to the actual fighting. Doctrinal differences made American carriers more capacious than the British, but much less survivable.

If the Hurricanes had had a hard time against the '109E, the '109F was even worse. Faster, more maneuvrable and with a better climb rate than its predecessor, the '109F completely outclassed the British fighter. In the first two months of 1942, Hurricane claims were 10, but their losses were 19!

Although radar and the Y-service gave the defenders a modicum of early warning, it was never long enough for them to gain sufficient altitude. In addition, Malta posed unique problems. The total area of the islands is only 120 sq miles (311 sq km); there was no space to be fancy. One obvious move was to gain height to the south, away from the direction of the threat, before coming back in, but often the German fighters were ready and waiting up-sun. The Axis fighters also learned to stagger their arrival in order to have pairs of Messerschmitts patrolling the airfield approaches when the defenders were short of fuel and trying to land.

It was soon obvious that the Hurricanes were fighting a losing battle, and on March 7 1942, the first 15 Spitfires were ferried to the beleaguered island. Alas they were too few to make much difference. In April, having "borrowed" the American carrier *Wasp*, 47 Spitfires arrived on Malta. Their arrival could not be concealed; the Luftwaffe reacted in force, and at the end of the following day only 18 remained serviceable.

Sixty more Spitfires followed in May; this time better organization saved them from being decimated in the air, and heavy fighting took place. Then fate intervened. The demands of other fronts led to the transfer of most Luftwaffe units from Sicily; the only remaining fighter units was II/JG 53. Almost overnight the situation reversed. The fighting was far from over, but the decisive moment had passed. It would never return.

Interestingly, the opposing top-scorers over Malta – German Gerhard Michalski and Canadian George Beurling – both claimed 26 victories over the island, flying at much the same time. But while Michalski generally held the initial advantage, Beurling operated in a far more target-rich environment.

TUNISIA

Even as Montgomery's victory at El Alamein set the scene for one of the longest retreats in history, the Allies, British and American this time, landed at the far end of the continent. Pushing forward, they caught the Axis forces in a classic pincer movement. The next few months saw them compressed into Tunisia.

As usual by this stage, the Luftwaffe was used as a fire brigade. First to arrive was II/JG 51 followed by II/JG 2, both with FW 190As, the first time these had been seen in North Africa. But caught between east and west, they were heavily outnumbered. They also had to face several new types: Spitfire IXs, A-36 Mustangs, and P-38 Lightnings. Allied top scorers in Tunisia were Spitfire pilot Neville Duke (14), and P-40 Warhawk pilot Levi Chase (10).

The Allied Offensive

1943-1945

Bristling with defensive guns, Boeing B-17Gs of the 381st Bomb Group set course for German targets. Daylight bombing was far more accurate than attacks at night, provided that the target could be found; not always easy in the cloud-laden skies of Western Europe.

THE NEED for a long-range escort fighter had been foreseen well before the war, and several nations had developed machines that they thought might serve. The problem was that to obtain sufficient range these airplanes were large, twin-engined, and generally, although not always, multiplace. The German Me 110 was a case in point. But having a fighter with sufficient range was not enough; it had to be able to hold its own against fast and agile enemy single-engined single-seaters. This was simply beyond the state of the art at that time.

By arming their bombers with powered turrets with multiple machine guns, the British theorized that the cross-fire of a close formation would be sufficient to defend it against fighter attack. Alas, once combat was joined, this theory was disproved. Losses became unsustainable, and apart from rare exceptions RAF Bomber Command was forced to switch to night raiding.

This caused problems, not the least of which was finding the target over a blacked-out Germany, let alone hitting it. While this resulted in a great deal of wasteful "agricultural"

bombing, it was at that time the only way of carrying the fight to Germany. Bomber Command persevered, continually seeking better means of navigation and target finding, but in general reduced to area bombing of strategic locations. In the interests of mass destruction, British bombers carried ever-heavier bomb loads and, as the war progressed, ever-larger bombs.

By contrast, the USAAF arrived in England late in 1942, firmly committed to precision bombing, carried out in daylight by massive formations. The British attempted to dissuade them, but the USAAF would not be moved. They had put a tremendous amount of resources into their doctrine of precision bombing, and they were determined to at least give it a try.

The main American bomber was the four-engined Boeing B-17, heavily defended against fighters by seven gun positions, with nine .50 caliber Brownings, which had far greater hitting power and were much longer-ranged than the .303s used by the RAF, plus a single .30 caliber gun in the nose. The warload of the B-17 was limited, as was the size of weapons that it carried, by the design of the bomb bay, but the

idea was that a few bombs accurately aimed would be far more effective than a heavier load dropped in the general target area.

The Jagdflieger were thus faced with a dual threat: RAF Bomber Command by night, the USAAF 8th Air Force by day. This combination alone posed some unique problems.

WHITE STAR BY DAY

To the defending German pilots, the American heavy bombers were very much an unknown, and rather fearsome quantity. Their sheer size was beyond the experience of the average pilot, and this caused extreme difficulties in judging distances. Many, fearful of a midair collision, broke off their attacks before reaching effective range. Only with practice did they become familiar with these four-engined giants, and better able to counter them.

The traditional fighter attack from astern was made amidst a hail of fire from the bomber gunners. Whilst their standard of marksmanship was not high, the sheer volume of fire was daunting. Many fighters were hit, even before they reached effective firing range. When on January 27 1943 B-17s first entered German air space, seven FW 190As were lost, for just three bombers. It was soon clear that this approach was unduly hazardous. Examination of shot-down B-17s revealed that the weakest area of defensive fire was directly ahead. The head-on attack was born.

The best British bomber of the war was the Avro Lancaster which carried a far greater bomb load than the USAAF heavies.

Head-on attacks by Luftwaffe fighters led to increased frontal armament. This B-17G has twin .50in Brownings in the remotely controlled chin turret, and two cheek-mounted Brownings.

Two squadrons of P-38 Lightnings carrying invasion stripes set off to carry the war to the enemy. Although the effect here is rather muddled, examination reveals that the lead unit is in finger fours; the second, and rather higher squadron is using a box formation.

This had several advantages. The combined speeds of bomber and fighter ensured that the latter were under fire only for a matter of seconds. While the firing time for the fighter was even shorter, the main target became the virtually unprotected front cockpit. Hits in this area were often lethal. The main difficulty was in lining up exactly head-on; even when this was achieved, a slight change of course by the bombers could throw it out.

One thing quickly became evident. It took an average of 20 hits with 20mm shells to bring down a heavy bomber, and this was rarely achieved in a single pass. What normally happened was that if a bomber was damaged enough to force it to leave the protection of its formation, it could be finished off later. But what was really needed was heavier weaponry, able to knock down a bomber in a single pass.

Experiments with air-to-air bombing and 8.25in (21cm) mortars carried underwing in launch tubes met limited success due to difficulties of accurate aiming. In the latter case, judging launch distance proved intractable,

while gravity drop with these weapons was about 200ft (61m). Also, the added weight and drag reduced performance and maneuvrability, and if escort fighters were present the German interceptors were severely handicapped.

THE FIRST ESCORTS

With the short-legged Spitfire demonstrably inadequate for the task, the USAAF had introduced its own, rather longer-ranged fighters. Whereas British engine manufacturers used two-stage supercharging to give high altitude performance, the Americans used turbo-supercharging. Air from the intake was ducted to the rather large turbo-supercharger, the turbine of which was driven by exhaust gases ducted from the engine. The intake air, having been compressed in the turbo-supercharger, was then ducted back to the engine aspiration system.

While the benefits of this system were undeniable, it was so heavy and bulky that it virtually demanded that the airframe be designed to suit. In 1937 Lockheed, attempting to meet a high performance specification, decided that a single-engined fighter using the best engine then available, the Allison V-1710 liquid-cooled engine, could not meet the requirements. By default they selected a twin-engined layout, and the twin-boom configuration used by what became the P-38 Lightning was adopted primarily to house the turbo-supercharger.

The Lightning was fast, but its twin engines, large span and high wing loading made it not very agile, even though combat flaps were fitted to later models to increase usable lift during heavy maneuvring. An odd feature for a fighter was a yoke control column rather than a stick. Armament consisted of one 20mm

The famous German 88mm anti-aircraft gun waits patiently for a target as searchlights probe the night sky. While AA guns caused a fair amount of damage, losses to this cause were infrequent.

Hispano cannon and four 12.7mm Brownings, all nose-mounted.

The Allisons were never very reliable, and this was a major fault of the type. Its combat debut was over Tunisia, where it was often forced to fight well below its best altitude. Against German fighters it was never a great success. It became available for escort duties in western Europe from October 1943, but a year later all Lightnings had been withdrawn from the escort groups, and they were widely used for strafing and close air support.

In 1940, the very powerful Pratt & Whitney Double Wasp 18-cylinder radial engine was selected for Republic Aviation's new fighter. This

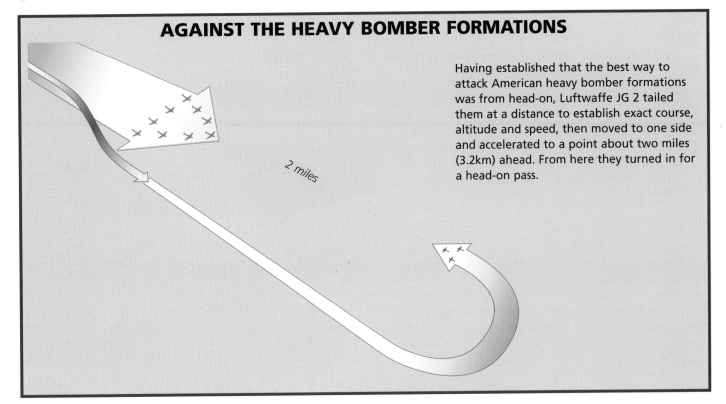

AGAINST THE HEAVY BOMBER FORMATIONS

2 miles

Having established that the best way to attack American heavy bomber formations was from head-on, Luftwaffe JG 2 tailed them at a distance to establish exact course, altitude and speed, then moved to one side and accelerated to a point about two miles (3.2km) ahead. From here they turned in for a head-on pass.

Adversaries! From this angle it is easy to see how mistakes were made. Nearest the camera is a captured FW 190A in British markings, while beside it is a P-47B Thunderbolt. Side-on they appear very similar.

109G and the FW 190A. The standing joke was that the only way to take evasive action was to undo the straps and run around the cockpit.

But when action was joined, its pilots found that it had virtues all of its own. Finely harmonized controls gave it a very fast rate of roll, which in part compensated for its mediocre turning ability. This was put to good use by some P-47 aces, notably Bob Johnson, who often used three-dimensional rolling maneuvers to gain a firing position against a better-turning opponent. In a dive the Jug could even outpace the FW 190A. Its armament of eight wing-mounted .50in Brownings gave it a very heavy punch, and it could survive an amazing amount of battle damage.

Even with drop-tanks, the early Thunderbolts could barely reach the German border. All the Jagdflieger had to do was wait until the bombers passed beyond the range of their escorts before attacking. This is what happened on August 17 1943, when American bombers set course for Schweinfurt. Of 363 heavies, 60 were shot down and many more badly damaged. Then, when on October 14 the US 8th AF returned to Schweinfurt, another 60 were shot down and 138 suffered moderate to severe damage. These were victories for the fighter defenses. The writing was on the wall for the unescorted bomber formation.

offered enough power for a single-engined layout, and the turbo-supercharger was located in the fuselage behind the pilot. This involved a tremendous amount of ducting to lead air and gases back and forth, and the airframe of what became the P-47 Thunderbolt was designed around it. By any standards the P-47, promptly called the Juggernaut, or Jug, was huge; it could hardly have been otherwise.

Operational over western Europe from April 1943, "the seven-ton milk bottle", as it was derisorily called, at first looked a loser. It was outclimbed and out-turned by both the Me

Gradually the reach of the Thunderbolt was extended, using drop tanks under the wings as well as beneath the fuselage, while the Lightning, despite its faults, could range even deeper into Germany. Then finally, in December 1943, the greatest escort fighter of them all entered the fray.

This was the P-51 Mustang, powered by a license-built Rolls-Royce Merlin engine. A low-drag design with a laminar flow wing, the Mustang could cruise farther and faster on the same amount of fuel as the similarly-engined

REPUBLIC P-47D THUNDERBOLT

Dimensions: Span 40ft 9in (12.42m); Length 36ft 1in (11m); Height 14ft 2in (4.32m); Wing area 300sq.ft (27.87m²).
Power: One Pratt & Whitney R-2800-59 Double Wasp 18-cylinder turbocharged radial engine rated at 2,300hp.
Weights: Empty 10,700lb (4,853kg); Loaded 14,600lb (6,623kg).
Performance: Maximum speed 429mph (690km/hr); Ceiling 40,000ft (12,191m); Climb (initial) 2,780ft/min (14.12m/sec); Range 950 miles (1,529km).
Armament: Eight .50 caliber (12.7mm) wing-mounted Browning machine guns.

First flown on May 6 1941, the Thunderbolt was huge; the largest single-seat single-engined fighter of the war. The quest for high altitude performance called for turbocharging, and this and the associated ducting determined its size. It became operational with 56th

Fighter Group in April 1943, when it was promptly dubbed the Juggernaut, quickly shortened to Jug. Whilst it could be outclimbed and out-turned by the opposing German fighters, it had virtues of its own. It could out-dive them, rate of roll was surprisingly fast, it packed a tremendous punch, and was tough. Most of the American aces in Europe flew the Jug at one time or another, and all ten of the top P-47 aces survived the war.

NORTH AMERICAN P-51D MUSTANG

Dimensions: Span 37ft (11.28m);
Length 32ft 3in (9.83m); Height 13ft 8in (4.17m);
Wing area 233sq.ft (21.65m^2).
Power: One Packard-Merlin V-1650-7 liquid-cooled
V-12 engine rated at 1,695hp.
Weights: Empty 7,635lb (3,463kg);
Loaded 10,100lb (4,581kg).
Performance: Maximum speed 437mph (703km/hr);
Ceiling 40,000ft (12,191m); Climb (initial) 3,475ft/min
(17.65m/sec); Range (with drop tanks) 2,080 miles
(3,347km).
Armament: Six .50 caliber (12.7mm) wing-mounted
Browning machine guns.

Initially commissioned for the RAF, this American fighter
was at first powered by the Allison V-1710 engine.
Aerodynamically very clean, with a low-drag laminar-flow
wing, it lacked high altitude performance. Re-engined
with the Rolls-Royce Merlin, it became the best long
range fighter of the war, able to escort American heavy
bombers all the way to Berlin. The original P-51B was
armed with just four 12.7mm Brownings, and these often
jammed during heavy maneuvring. The later P-51D, fitted
with a tear-drop canopy to give a first-class all-round

view, was slightly slower, but was armed with six heavy
machine guns. In combat the Mustang was a match for
any of its German or Japanese opponents, and it
comfortably outranged them all.

Spitfire IX. Given fuel tanks in the wing roots, a
large extra tank in the rear fuselage, and drop
tanks, the Mustang could go all the way to
Berlin, which it first did in March 1944. No
longer could the German fighters wait until the
bombers passed beyond the range of their
escorts; they were now faced with escorted
bombers everywhere!

LUFTWAFFE DILEMMA

The Luftwaffe was now caught on the horns of a
dilemma. To halt the damaging daylight raids
they needed to inflict far greater attrition, and to
do this they needed much greater hitting power.

Aerial bombing and 8.25in (21cm) mortars had
failed; the only possible answer was heavier
guns. But the larger the gun, the slower the rate
of fire and the fewer the hits scored. The head-
on attack gave little firing time; the alternative
was to approach more slowly from astern,
having armored their fighters against the
defensive crossfire.

More and bigger guns, coupled with greater
protection, meant increased weight, and
increased weight meant reduced performance.
The FW 190A-8/R8 Sturmbock carried two
30mm MK 108 cannon in underwing gondolas,
two 20mm MG 151s in the wing roots, and two

The North American
P-51D Mustang was
the best USAAF fighter
of the war. A Rolls-
Royce engine married
to an American
airframe with a
supercritical wing,
produced a long-range
escort fighter able to
range the length and
breadth of the Third
Reich.

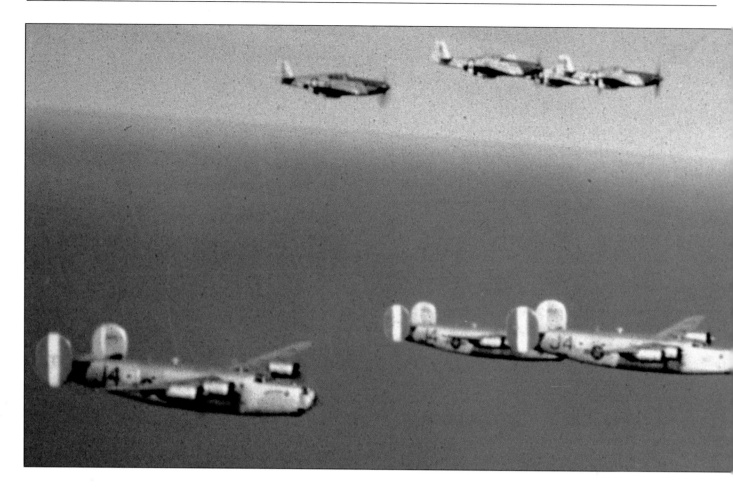

nose-mounted 12.7mm machine guns. Extra armor protected the engine, cockpit, and magazines, while bullet-proof glass was scabbed on to the cockpit transparencies. All this extra weight and drag reduced performance and made handling sluggish. The paradox was that in making the fighters less vulnerable to the crossfire from the bombers, the Luftwaffe had made them more vulnerable to the escort fighters.

To overcome this, the Gefechtsverband, about 100 fighters in all, was introduced. This consisted of a heavily armed and armored Sturmgruppe, escorted by two Gruppen of conventional fighters whose task was to protect the Sturmgruppe from the escort fighters.

On the rare occasions when it worked, this was devastating. On July 7 1944, 23 B-24 Liberators were shot from the sky. Nine German fighters were lost and three more force-landed. But more often it could not be done; the escort fighters ranged ahead and on the flanks of the bombers, intercepting and breaking up the huge German formation before it could make contact.

ESCORT TACTICS

In the early days, the American fighters were tied closely to the bombers, reacting only when their charges came under threat. Like the Jagdwaffe in 1940 they found this a handicap, and as experience grew were released to rove

Consolidated B-24 Liberators escorted by P-51 Mustangs. A later design than the B-17, the B-24 was faster, but had a lower ceiling and was more difficult to fly in close formation.

Above: The P-51D differed from the P-51B in having a cut-down rear fuselage with a bubble canopy for all-round good view, and six .50 machine guns instead of four. The guns had been redesigned to reduce jamming.

Left: The P-51B was the first Merlin-engined Mustang. View from the cockpit was inferior, and the four wing-mounted guns tended to jam during hard maneuvring.

ahead and on the flanks of the bombers, typically in fours and eights, all prepared to reinforce each other at need.

Control was the greatest problem. Cruising speeds of bombers and fighters varied widely. On a deep penetration the escorts could not fly all the way to the target in company with the bombers, but were forced to operate in relays. Thunderbolts took the first legs; Lightnings the next, with Mustangs at extreme range. This called for fine timing. Often the bomber stream was 90 miles(145km) long, and it was virtually impossible to give it cover everywhere all of the time.

Colonel Don Blakeslee, arguably the greatest American fighter leader of the war, was on one occasion given overall control of the entire escort force, several hundred fighters. But one man, in the confined cockpit of a Mustang with

inadequate communications for the task, could do little outside his immediate area. The responsibility remained with the Fighter Group commander on the spot.

By late 1944, German pilot losses had become insupportable. The small band of "old heads", individually very capable, melted away in the furnace of combat. Their replacements were generally undertrained and inexperienced; easy meat for the aggressive American fighter pilots. Allied losses fell; even RAF Bomber Command once more started attacking in daylight.

ROUNDELS BY NIGHT

By the end of 1942, the Luftwaffe had developed a belt of defensive boxes, each with tight ground control, each patrolled by one or two radar-equipped night fighters. The main problem was that the RAF had adopted the bomber stream, passing all airplanes rapidly through the defensive belt on a narrow frontage. The effect of this was that only a fraction of the available night fighters could be brought into action against any one raid.

Night operations were extremely dependent on electronic aids. They were used by ground control to direct fighters, by fighters to find the bombers, and by bombers to navigate, to find their targets, and to detect attacking fighters.

This gave rise to a whole new art: electronic warfare (EW). For the most part, EW consisted of jamming. Radar jamming made the night fighter electronically blind, while communications jamming hindered effective ground control. There was however another aspect. Radar

Aerodynamic forces exerted on an out of control bomber were enormous. This American B-17, with elevators shot away and structure weakened by battle damage has shed a wing as it spirals to destruction.

Cover of darkness was lost over the target. Huge fires on the ground, searchlights, and flak, combined to silhouette the raiders, such as this RAF Lancaster over Hamburg on January 30 1943.

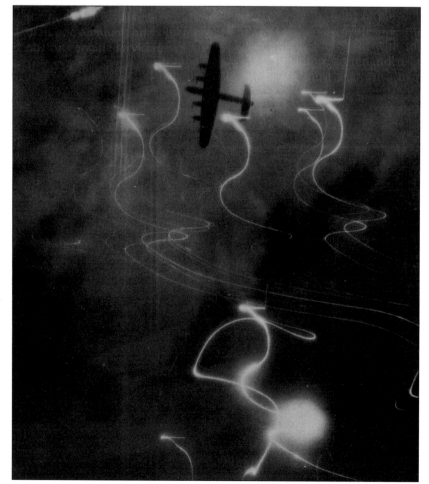

emissions could be homed upon, giving direction and positive identification, if not actual range. Both sides used this – the Germans to find the bombers, the British intruders to find the German night fighters.

It had long been known that chaff, foil strips cut to half the radar wavelength, would give a host of spurious echoes on the radar screen, making it all but impossible for the real targets to

be detected. It was first used on July 23/24 1943. German early warning radar detected a large force of bombers over the North Sea. Then, with little warning, the echoes from several hundred bombers suddenly multiplied to 11,000!

Swamped, the German detection and control system collapsed, and Hamburg was heavily bombed. Further raids using chaff followed. Bereft of night fighter control, the Nachtjagdflieger were forced to revert to simpler means.

While chaff hid individual bombers in a mass of false radar returns, the presence of the bomber stream could not be disguised. The night fighters were scrambled, and sent to orbit a radio beacon. From here they were directed towards the bomber stream. There, they flew and fought until low on fuel; then, like the day fighters, they landed at the nearest airfield to replenish, and took off again, returning home only in the cold light of dawn. This was the Nachtjagdfliegers' migratory period.

Ranking night fighter Experte Heinz-Wolfgang Schnaufer (121 victories), specialized in heading for the area where the jamming was thickest, there to search visually. Once there, he was aided by the remarkable night vision of his gunner, Wilhelm Gänsler, with whom he shared 98 victories, and an almost telepathic understanding with radar operator Fritz Rumpelhardt.

WILDE SAU

The area bombing of the RAF caused enormous fires on the ground, against which later-arriving bombers were silhouetted. This was turned to advantage by using day fighters, Me 109s and FW 190As, at night. In theory the flak ceiling was limited, allowing the fighters to operate above it, but this did not always work. As always a handful of pilots achieved above average results. The most successful Wilde Sau pilot was

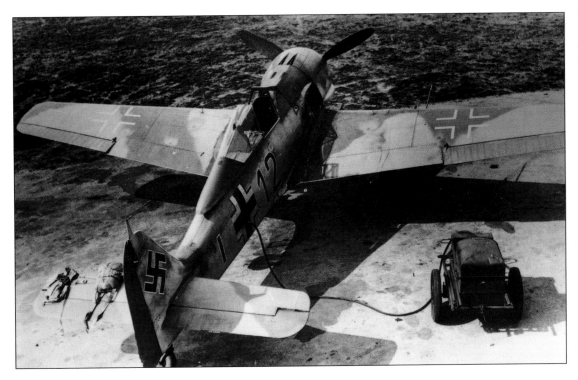

The Focke-Wulf FW 190A was a day fighter used at night for the Wilde Sau mission. It was not a great success, as operational attrition was high. In adverse weather, many pilots were unable to find their way back to base, while others crashed on landing.

Nasen Muller, a former airline pilot, with 23 victories. Wilde Sau was moderately effective during the summer of 1943 but, with the onset of winter weather, operational attrition due to accidents rose to prohibitive levels.

NIGHT FIGHTERS

The main German night fighters throughout the war were the Me 110 which, increasingly loaded with equipment, ended with barely enough performance to catch the bombers, and the Junkers Ju 88, which in the final year was the pre-eminent type. Just one other was brought into service, the Heinkel He 219 Uhu, but not in any great numbers.

The He 219 had, on paper at least, an impressive performance. Unfortunately the brochure figures could not be matched by the hardware, while wing loading (70lb/sq.ft) (344kg/m^2) was high, making it unmaneuvrable. While several top-scoring Experten, among them Helmut Lent, Heinz Rökker, Paul Zorner, Martin Becker, and Gerhardt Raht, all flew the Uhu, only 268 were built.

Standard procedure in night fighting was to approach low, where the fighter was masked against the dark ground, then swim up from the depths to attack. The risk was that as it did so it would be seen by the bomber's rear gunner. At the ranges normal in night attacks, four .303in Brownings in a powered turret were deadly.

The German answer to this problem was Schräge Musik – upward-firing cannon mounted at a 60 degree angle. This enabled the fighter to formate unseen below the bomber before unleashing a deadly burst of fire. While this

Widely regarded as the best Luftwaffe night fighter of the war, the Heinkel He 219 Uhu. Performance failed to match the brochure figures, while the wing loading was extremely high. It was no match for the RAF Mosquito.

Pilot and observer of the Mosquito F.II night fighter sat side by side behind a flat bullet-proof windscreen. This aircraft, DD750 of RAF No.25 sqn, flew into a hill, on night patrol, near Keighley, Yorkshire, on March 22 1943.

accounted for many British bombers, Schnaufer commented after the war that he had made only between 20 and 30 Schräge Musik attacks in his 121 victories, although less experienced pilots used this method almost exclusively.

ROUNDELS RAMPANT

The British had always held a lead in electronic warfare. In the summer of 1943, they introduced a device called Serrate, which homed on German night fighter radar emissions. As it gave no indications of range, it had to be used in conjunction with airborne radar (AI). It made its combat debut with the Beaufighters of 141 Squadron, commanded by Bob Braham, one of the most aggressive men

ever to strap a fighter on to his back.

Decisive combats between fighter aces in daylight were rare, and at night much more so. Braham, using Serrate in the almost obsolescent Beaufighter, accounted for no fewer than three Experten at night – Georg Kraft (14), Heinz Vinke (54), and August Geiger (53) – in his total of 29 destroyed and two probables.

By 1944 the superb Mosquito had almost entirely supplanted the Beaufighter, and ranged the length and breadth of Germany, hunting down the Nachtjagdflieger. The German pilots knew that they were under threat from the moment that their wheels started to roll on takeoff until they stopped after landing. The ultimate in EW was reached with Perfectos, a

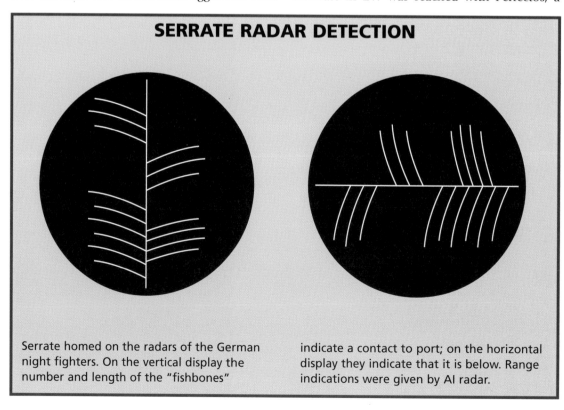

SERRATE RADAR DETECTION

Serrate homed on the radars of the German night fighters. On the vertical display the number and length of the "fishbones"

indicate a contact to port; on the horizontal display they indicate that it is below. Range indications were given by AI radar.

device which triggered the German identification friend/foe. It announced in effect, "I am a German night fighter; this is where I am and this is what I am doing." In the final seven months of the war NJG 4 lost about 50 fighters. Of these, five fell to return fire from bombers, 30 to the ubiquitous Mosquitos, and 15 to unknown causes.

The leading Mosquito night fighter pilot of the war was Branse Burbridge of 85 Squadron who, with his radar operator Bill Skelton, was credited with 21 victories, 16 over enemy territory. On the night of June 14/15 1944 they shot down a Ju 188 night fighter flown by Experte Wilhelm Herget (72 victories). On November 4/5 they scored four victories over Germany.

BUILD-UP TO INVASION

Even before the Hurricane entered service, Hawker Aircraft started to plan its successor around a new and far more powerful engine, the Napier Sabre, with its 24 cylinders arranged in an H-form. First flown on February 24 1940, this was the Typhoon, which entered service in September 1941. It was however dogged by engine and structural failures, and the definitive variant was the Typhoon Ib, which had a redesigned fuselage with a bubble canopy and four wing-mounted 20mm Hispano cannon.

Although fast enough to catch the low level "tip and run" FW 190 raiders in 1943, the Typhoon was not very agile, while its high altitude performance and handling left much to be desired. Only one pilot reached double figures with the Typhoon; this was Johnny Baldwin, who claimed 15 victories. All except two were Me 109Gs or FW 190As. The true metier of the Typhoon was close air support and

tank-busting, where it gained an enviable reputation. Meanwhile a thinner elliptical wing of greater area was designed; a fuselage tank replaced those in the wings, and the tail surfaces were enlarged. Thus modified, the Typhoon became the Tempest V, one of the best medium and low level fighters of the war. Tempest top-scorer was David "Foob" Fairbanks, with 11 victories out of his war total of 12.

Successor to the Hurricane, the Typhoon was fast, heavily armed with four 20mm Hispano cannon, but lacked high altitude performance and agility. But armed with bombs or rockets, it was unsurpassed in the close air support role.

The Typhoon was powered by the Napier Sabre 24-cylinder engine, the huge air intake of which often caused it to be mistaken for the FW 190. The thick wing seen here was replaced by a thinner wing on the Tempest to give a first-class fighter.

By the midwar period, the Merlin engine was fast reaching the limits of development, and Rolls-Royce designed the much more powerful and only slightly larger Griffon to replace it. The Spitfire VIII airframe was extensively modified to accept the new engine, and the result was the Spitfire XIV, which entered service in January 1944. Not as pleasant handling as early variants, it was very fast and extremely potent.

As the date for Operation Overlord, the invasion of Normandy, drew near, the Allies made a massive bid for air supremacy, flying nearly three times as many fighter sorties as the Luftwaffe. Fighter-bombers, Typhoons, Spitfires, Lightnings, Thunderbolts and Mustangs roamed the skies over northern France seeking targets of opportunity.

OVERLORD AND AFTER

On D-Day, June 6 1944, Allied fighters threw an almost impenetrable air umbrella over the beachhead, and followed this with an all-out assault. During the next three months they averaged more than 1,600 sorties a day, outnumbering the Jagdwaffe in the air by 6:1 and inflicting 3,527 losses, many of which were destroyed on the ground. Allied fighter losses during this period were just 561 to all causes, a mere quarter of a per cent in terms of sorties.

Harried from temporary landing ground to temporary landing ground, the Luftwaffe lost all cohesion. Not until after summer, when the Allied armies outran their supply lines and were forced to halt, did they manage to reorganize.

One outstanding German fighter entered service at this time. This was the Focke-Wulf FW 190D-9 Dora, generally called the "long-nose" by Allied pilots. It differed from the FW 190A in several respects. It was powered by a Junkers Jumo 213A liquid-cooled engine, with an annular radiator which gave the appearance of being a radial. Other changes were a longer fuselage and an enlarged vertical tail.

Transient performance (roll and pitch) was a bit slower than in the FW 190A but the Dora was faster, climbed and dived better, and in a hard turn did not bleed off speed so quickly. Generally superior to the Lightning and Thunderbolt, and to a degree the Mustang, it was slightly inferior in performance to the Spitfire XIV and Tempest V, while both British fighters could comfortably out-turn it. But flown by a good pilot, it was a formidable foe.

RAF Mustangs over an Allied armored force, Falaise, August 1944. Allied air superiority was at this time almost total, allowing ground forces to move freely.

Developed from the Typhoon, the Tempest V was the most potent Allied fighter at low and medium levels.

DAY FIGHTER COMPARISONS, EUROPE 1943-1945

Type	Speed (mph/km-hr	Ceiling(ft/m)	Climb	Range(ml/km)
Supermarine Spitfire XIV	448/721	44,500/13,563	4,580ft/min (23.27m/sec)	460/740
Hawker Tempest V	435/700	36,000/10,972	4,700ft/min (23.87m/sec)	740/1,191
Messerschmitt Me 163B Komet	596/959	53,972/16,450	3min 21sec to 39,372ft (12000m)	Endurance 10 min.
Focke-Wulf FW 190A-8	408/657	37,403/11,400	9min 54sec to 20,014ft (6,100m)	497/800
Hawker Typhoon Ib	412/663	35,200/10,728	5min 54 sec to 15,000ft (4,572m)	980/821
Lockheed P-38 Lightning	390/628	40,000/12,191	7min to 20,000ft (6,096m)	2,260/3,637

FOCKE-WULF FW 190D-9

Dimensions: Span 34ft 5½ in (10.50m);
Length 33ft 5¼ in (10.24m);
Height 11ft (3.35m);
Wing area 197sq.ft (18.30m^2).
Power: One Junkers Jumo 213A water-cooled
engine with water-methanol injection rated
at 2,240hp.
Weights: Empty 7,694lb (3,590kg);
Loaded 9,480lb (4,300kg).
Performance: Maximum speed 426mph
(685km/hr); Ceiling 39,372ft (12,000m);
Climb 16 min 48sec to 32,810ft (10,000m);
Range 520 miles (837km).
Armament: Two MG 151/20 wing-mounted
cannon and two 12.7mm MG 131 nose-
mounted machine guns.

The FW 190D Dora, known to the Allies as the "long-nose", varied from the earlier variants in having a liquid-cooled engine, but with an annular radiator which made it look like a radial. Other differences were a stretched fuselage and larger tail surfaces. The Dora entered large-scale service in the autumn of 1944, and was at first greeted with suspicion. Roll rate was slower than the FW 190A, and it was sluggish in the pitching plane, but it accelerated faster and climbed and dived better than its predecessor. Although superior to the Thunderbolt and Mustang, it was in some ways inferior to the latest British fighters: the Spitfire XIV and the Tempest V. This notwithstanding, it was treated with great respect by the Allied fighters.

THE LUFTWAFFE'S LAST THROW

Desperate to halt the American daylight bombing, even if only temporarily, German fighter general Adolph Galland had tried to build up sufficient force to strike a decisive blow. It was not to be. Many fighters were frittered away while supporting the unsuccessful Ardennes campaign. The remainder, about 800 in all, were launched against Allied airfields at dawn on January 1 1945, in Operation Bodenplatte. It was a disaster.

Luftwaffe airplane losses were much heavier than those of the Allies but, to make matters worse, 237 German pilots went down, many of them experienced leaders. It is a truism of warfare that air forces run out of pilots more quickly than they run out of airplanes. The Jagdflieger never recovered from this setback.

The bitter fighting in support of the ground forces during the final ten months of the war saw few aces emerge. For the most part the few experienced German pilots were overwhelmed by sheer numbers, and spent most of their time evading, while for the Allies it was lack of opportunity. Just a few beat the odds, but even Johnnie Johnson, the greatest British Wing Leader of the war, only managed to add ten to his impressive tally. Of the six who reached double figures, five of them, including Johnnie Johnson, flew the Spitfire IX.

The most potent Spitfire of the war was the Mk XIV with the Rolls-Royce Griffon engine. Performance was far superior to earlier variants, but handling was less pleasant, due to increased weight.

In an attempt to counter Allied air power the Luftwaffe introduced an austere mass-produced jet, the Heinkel He 162. It was however tricky to fly, and like most other panic measures, it was a failure.

The only British jet fighter to enter service in the war was the Gloster Meteor. Only a handful saw action, and the type was never engaged in air combat, although Meteors destroyed several German aircraft on the ground.

Fairbanks, previously mentioned, was top-scorer with the Tempest, while Harry Walmsley accounted for nine with the Spitfire XIV, eight of them between March 13 and April 25 1945, to make his final total 11.

THE JETS

With the internal combustion engine, power has to be converted into thrust by the propeller, but the higher the speed, the less efficient this method becomes. So greatly did maximum speeds increase during the war that, towards its end, the piston engine was nearing its practical limits. For further progress to be possible, a different system was needed: a reaction motor, in which the thrust was created directly.

There were two basic possibilities: the rocket motor, which although simple in principle, demanded exotic and dangerous fuels in enormous quantities, and the gas turbine or jet engine, far more complex, and needing special high-temperature metals. Germany attacked the problem from both directions, and actually succeeded in putting jet and rocket-powered

The Gloster E28/39, first ever British jet airplane. First flown in May 1941, development of the engine to give power enough for a fighter took a considerable time.

fighters into operational service, albeit in small numbers.

The advantage of the rocket motor was that an enormous amount of power could be generated from a very small engine. On the other hand, whereas both reciprocating and jet engines drew oxygen from the air through which they flew, the rocket had to carry its own oxidant. This severely curtailed endurance, and to get adequate performance the airframe had to be as small and light as possible. On the other hand, decreasing back-pressure on the rocket chamber meant that unlike with conventional aspirated airplanes performance actually increased with altitude.

ROCKET FIGHTER

The Messerschmitt Me 163B Komet was a tail-less airplane with a moderately swept wing. It carried 405 US gal(1,534 liters) of fuel; two thirds of it highly unstable and corrosive high-test (90 per cent solution) hydrogen peroxide. The Walter HWK 109 bifuel motor gave the Komet a maximum speed of 596mph (959km/hr), and an almost incredible 2min 36sec to reach 39,372ft (12,000m). On the other hand, endurance under power was a mere eight minutes, and operational radius was less than 50 miles (80km). It was armed with two 30mm Mauser MK108 cannon with 60 rounds each. As a weight-saving measure, it took off from a jettisonable trolley, and landed back on a retractable skid.

In theory, the Komet was an excellent point defense interceptor, able to be held on the ground until the American bomber formations were sighted, and only then scrambled. It climbed fast, it intercepted, avoiding the escort fighters by sheer speed. With all fuel expended, it then glided back to base. This was not quite as suicidal as it sounds; even without power it could be safely dived at more than 500mph (805km/hr), and at speeds of more than 250mph (402km/hr) it was remarkably agile.

In practice things were not this easy. By its very nature, it needed clear weather to be effective, and this was rarely the case. With the rocket motor running it left a thick trail of smoke across the sky, making it visible from miles away, thus forfeiting the advantage of surprise. Landing speed was high, and the landing approach had to be perfect; there was no second chance. Finally, the volatile nature of the fuels frequently caused explosions, and the Komet killed more of its own pilots than it ever did the enemy.

A point defense interceptor intended to counter the American heavy bomber fleets, the Messerschmitt Me 163 Komet was the world's first rocket-propelled fighter. The first Komet sortie was flown on August 16 1944.

JET FIGHTER

Several German jet fighters were flown before the end of the war, including the Heinkel He 280, notable for the first recorded use of the ejection seat to save the pilot. But only one saw any appreciable operational service. This was the Messerschmitt Me 262 Schwalbe.

Powered by two Junkers Jumo 109-004B axial-flow turbojets, the Me 262 was in all other ways conventional. The engines were mounted outboard on the wings, where they would have been had the Me 262 been a propeller-driven type. Had they been positioned inboard, problems of assymetric handling with one engine out could have been avoided, and rate of roll improved. No attempt was made to improve pilot view by moving the cockpit forward, ahead of the wings, which it could so easily have been. But this is with hindsight. All things considered, it was still a superb fighter.

Operationally it was difficult to utilize. Its overwhelming speed was vital for evading the escorts, but embarrassing when attacking bombers, since even in the traditional approach from astern little time was available to line up, aim and fire, before being forced to break away to avoid colliding with the target. But when it did connect, its armament of four 30mm Mauser MK108 cannon was devastating.

Like all early jet engines, response time of the Jumos was slow. Once up to speed it was best to leave the throttles alone during combat, and retard them only when it was time to land. Inattention to turbine temperatures easily resulted in the engines catching fire. In any case, metallurgy was behind the state of the art, making the engines very short-lived.

Wing loading, at 60lb/sq.ft (293kg/m²), was high, and this, coupled with the speed, meant that the Me 262 could not turn tightly. If reefed around hard, it bled off speed at an alarming rate and, as acceleration was slow, it quickly

MESSERSCHMITT Me 262 SCHWALBE

Dimensions: Span 40ft 11½in (12.48m); Length 34ft 9½in (10.60m); Height 12ft 7in (3.87m); Wing area 234sq.ft (21.74m²).
Power: Two Junkers Jumo 109-004 axial-flow turbojets rated at 1,980lb (898kg) static thrust.
Weights: Empty 9,742lb (4,419kg); Loaded 14,101lb (6,396kg).
Performance: Maximum speed 541mph (870km/hr); Ceiling 37,565ft (37,576ft (11,450m); Climb (initial) 3,937ft/min (20m/sec); Range 526 miles (846km).
Armament: Four 30mm Mauser MK 108 cannon; two with 100 rpg; two with 80 rpg.

First flown in April 1941, the Schwalbe was the first jet fighter to be used operationally, although not until the late summer of 1944. Its overwhelming speed was a double-edged sword. It made the Me 262 almost uninterceptable by conventional fighters, but it made attacking much slower bombers very difficult by reducing the time available to line up and fire. Any attempt at hard maneuvring bled off speed at an alarming rate, making the Me 262 vulnerable to counter-attack, while the 30mm cannon, destructive though it was when a shell hit, had a low muzzle velocity, making it a close-range weapon. Never available in sufficient numbers, the Me 262 made less impact on the war than its performance warranted.

became vulnerable to conventional fighters. Maneuver combat had to be avoided. Nor could a steep diving attack be used without exceeding the limiting Mach number.

The other great weakness of the Me 262 was its short endurance, typically less than an hour. Aerodynamically very clean, the German jet lost speed very slowly, and the landing approach had to be very long and very straight. Aware of this, Allied fighters took to patrolling the approaches of known jet airfields in the hope of catching them while vulnerable.

A jet unit composed entirely of Experten, JV 44, was formed in April 1945, under the command of Adolph Galland. But by this time the war was irretrievably lost, and the elite unit achieved little.

A handful of German Experten reached double figures flying the Me 262. Pre-eminent among them was Heinz Baer, with 16 victories, a record which, although equalled in Korea, was not beaten until 1973, by an Israeli.

Both the RAF and USAAF flew jet fighters during the war – the British Gloster Meteor and the American Lockheed Shooting Star, but neither of these engaged in air combat.

The prototype Heinkel He 280 takes off on its first flight on April 2 1941, minus the engine cowlings, omitted because the jet engines leaked fuel. Notable for the first ever emergency ejection, the He 280 failed to enter service.

The first ever jet aircraft to fly was the Heinkel He 178, on August 27 1939. The early German lead in turbojet technology was lost due to the lack of suitable high temperature metals.

Naval Air Power

1941-1945

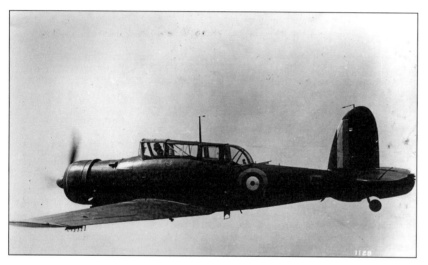

Safe operation from a carrier deck was the main consideration for the Blackburn Skua, which doubled as an air defense fighter and dive bomber. Against land-based aircraft, both its performance and armament were inadequate.

THE FIRST carrier-based fighters in action in the Second World War were British. For most of the inter-war years, the airplanes were controlled by the RAF; not until May 1939 did they revert to the Fleet Air Arm. As a result, carrier fighters were acquired on the basis of how safe they were to fly from ships, rather than how good they were for their tasks. Consequently they were much inferior to their land-based counterparts.

At the outbreak of war, the primary FAA fighter was the Sea Gladiator biplane. The first monoplane fighter was the Blackburn Skua, a two-seater which doubled as a divebomber. Slow, and with a pathetic rate of climb, the Skua was armed with four wing-mounted .303in (7.7mm) Browning machine guns, and a rear Lewis gun operated by the second crew member.

Most Skua operations took place off the coast of Norway in 1939/40. While it proved effective in driving off reconnaissance airplanes and shadowers, poor performance and lack of hitting power prevented many victories being scored. Top-scoring Skua pilot William Lucy shared in the destruction of seven twin-engined

bombers before being killed by return fire from Heinkel He 111s on May 14 1940.

The Fleet Air Arm for long insisted that its fighters needed a navigator for long overwater patrols. This built-in "headwind" was perpetuated in the Fairey Fulmar, which entered service in June 1940. Based on the Battle light bomber, its performance was better than that of the Skua, although still very much inferior to contemporary land-based fighters. But armed with eight wing-mounted .303in(7.7mm) Browning machine guns, it at least packed a hefty punch.

The Fulmar saw most action against the Regia Aeronautica while escorting convoys through the Mediterranean to Malta, and were moderately successful against Italian torpedo-bombers. Top-scorers were Stan Orr and Bill Barnes of 806 Squadron, and Rupert Tillard of 808 Squadron, with six each. All were multi-engined types except one Fiat CR.42 shot down by Orr.

The inadequacies of the Fulmar led to the navalization of the Hurricane and Spitfire, but these lacked the endurance to be fully effective as a fleet fighter, while the latter was in any case too delicate for deck-landing. American carrier fighters, such as the Wildcat, known to the British as the Martlet, then later the Hellcat and Corsair, were acquired by the Fleet Air Arm.

The final venture into the field of single-engined two-seaters was the Fairey Firefly. Powered by a Rolls-Royce Griffon engine, and armed with four 20mm Hispano cannon, it was far better than the Fulmar, but for interception and air combat, it was mediocre, and achieved little.

HMS *Formidable* was one of the new class of British carriers with an armored flight deck. This made them far more survivable if slightly less seaworthy than the fleet carriers of the US Navy. Here the forward lift is seen ascending.

THE FAR EAST

When the Japanese offensive burst like a tidal wave across the Far East and the Pacific, the capability of her fighters came as a nasty shock to the Allies. It should not have done; the Japanese had been in action against China, and to a lesser degree the Soviet Union, during the 1930s, while Claire Chennault, the commander of the American Volunteer Group in China, had already encountered them and devized suitable tactics against them.

Japanese fighter doctrine was to defeat the enemy in the air wherever they could be found, and to this end, dogfighting was the means employed. For this, maneuvrability was the primary requirement. Japanese aero-engines were no great shakes, and to compensate for lack of power airframes were built as light as possible, thus increasing power loading and minimizing wing loading. This was not done at the expense of structural strength – the Zero and Oscar could pull as much g as their western

A Fleet Air Arm Martlet approaches the deck of HMS *Illustrious* as the deck landing officer, usually known as 'bats', watches. The arrester hook is down, ready to catch one of the wires which can be seen across the deck.

Mitsubishi A6M2 Zero fighters warm up on the deck of the carrier *Hiryu* before the attack on Pearl Harbor. No fewer than six carriers took part in this raid, which caused mass destruction to the US Pacific Fleet and USAAF land-based units. These Zeros carry drop tanks to extend their endurance.

opponents – but such essentials as armor protection, self-sealing for fuel tanks, and even radios, were omitted. Consequently they were very vulnerable to hits; the clever bit was in scoring hits on such agile machines while flying a less maneuvrable fighter.

The other Japanese advantage lay in experience. Fighting over China had been hard, and in some ways encounters with the Russian I-153s, and particularly with the heavily armed and armored, but still very agile I-16s over Nomonghan, had been even harder. When in December 1941 they entered the Second World War, Japan possessed a cadre of very experienced and battle-hardened fighter pilots.

At the end of 1941, the RAF in the Far East, as it had been in Egypt, was equipped with second-rate fighters, of which the Hurricane was the best. The others were Curtiss Mohawks (Hawk 75s as used by the French in 1939) and Brewster Buffaloes. The latter was a real clunker; slow, with a poor rate of climb, sluggish in pitch and

MITSUBISHI A6M2 Model 21 ZERO

Dimensions: Span 39ft 4½in (12m);
Length 29ft 8½in (9.06m); Height 10ft (3.05m);
Wing area 242sq.ft (22.48m²).
Power: One Nakajima NK1C Sakae 14-cylinder aircooled radial engine rated at 950hp.
Weights: Empty 3,704lb (1,680kg);
Loaded 6,164lb (2,796kg).
Performance: Maximum speed 331mph (533km/hr); Ceiling 32,810ft (10,000m); Climb 7min 27sec to 19,685ft (6,000m); Range 1,161 miles(1,870km).
Armament: Two wing-mounted 20mm Type 99 cannon with 60 rpg; two nose-mounted 7.7mm Type 97 machine guns with 500 rpg.

The first American pilots to encounter the legendary Zero were impressed by its outstanding maneuvrability, which at normal combat speeds far outclassed their own fighters. Only later did they realize that the Japanese pilots paid a high price for this. While the Zero had been stressed for the usual combat maneuvers, it had been lightened by leaving off everything regarded as non-essential. This included armor protection, self-sealing fuel

tanks, and even the radio. As a direct result the Zero was very vulnerable, and could sustain little battle damage. Another failing was that as speed increased, rate of roll became progressively slower. The Zero was progressively upgraded throughout the war but, failing to keep pace with American fighter developments, was shot from the skies.

roll, and with an engine which showed a decided tendency to overheat. Not one of these airplanes could take on a Zero or a Ki-43 Hayabusa in a turning fight with any hope of winning, although, amazingly, Australian Alf Clare and New Zealander Geoffrey Fisken both claimed six victories against the Japanese while flying Buffaloes! Fisken went on to score a further five with the Kittyhawk.

WAR IN THE PACIFIC

The vast wastes of the Pacific, studded on its westernmost part by innumerable islands, posed unique problems in power projection, and made the aircraft carrier indispensable. The first blow was struck at Oahu in December 1941, when Japanese airplanes from six carriers made a surprise attack on the US Navy base at Pearl Harbor. A few Curtiss P-40s of the USAAF managed to get airborne, but were overwhelmed by sheer numbers. By great good fortune, all three USN carriers in the Pacific were away at the time.

For the next few months, Japanese forces swarmed in all directions – out across the Pacific islands; down the East Indies to New Guinea; across Malaya and Singapore – while in April 1942, a strong carrier force mounted a raid against Ceylon. Opposing Allied fighters, including the Dutch, were decimated. The inexperienced Allied pilots persisted in trying to dogfight with agile Zeros and Hayabusas, often flown by veterans of China.

The Zero in particular posed problems. Its inherent long range was increased by flying at minimum engine revolutions and hanging in the air just above the stall. This gave it an endurance of eight hours, enabling it to operate over distances previously considered impossible, and appear where it was least expected. Before long, the only effectives in the area were a handful of USAAF fighter squadrons, equipped with P-40 Tomahawks and P-39 Airacobras, the Royal Australian Air Force, mainly with Tomahawks, and the US Navy and Marine Corps with Grumman F4F Wildcats, carrier- and land-based.

The Wildcat, which bore the brunt of the Japanese onslaught for the next two years, was an extremely rugged fighter, which was just as well;

A huge explosion on the battleship USS *Arizona* forms a dramatic backdrop to damaged and burning USN aircraft at Ford Island. At first sight, the Japanese raid on Pearl Harbor appeared to be a great victory, but later events showed this was not the case.

The Grumman F4F Wildcat held the ring for the US Navy against the far more maneuvrable Zero for the first nine months of the Pacific War. It was tough and hard-hitting.

rolling plane. Consequently, once a Zero was committed to following it in a steep diving turn, the Wildcat could evade by reversing the turn, leaving the Japanese fighter unable to follow.

Tactically, the experienced Imperial Japanese Navy was far ahead of the Americans, but in part this was offset by American technical superiority. The American carriers had both radar and a fighter control system based on the British model of 1940. They also had an IFF and homing system, to enable their fighters to return to the carriers over the trackless wastes of the ocean, even though the carriers had changed their position by several tens of miles since takeoff.

Whereas land-based fighters tended to fly at high cruising speeds, carrier fighters worked on the assumption that while the enemy might rate 50 per cent, the sea rated 100 per cent. Unless operational considerations dictated otherwise, they flew at economical cruising speed, optimizing their endurance on the principle that at the end of the mission they would most probably have to search for the carrier, then await their turn to land. The disadvantage of this was that the low cruising speed made them more vulnerable to the surprise bounce.

A historic engagement took place in May 1942. This was the Battle of the Coral Sea, the first encounter between two fleets whose surface units never once sighted each other. An amphibious Japanese force sailed to capture Port Moresby, on the south coast of New Guinea, and

it was rather slower, was outclimbed, and easily out-turned by the Zero. However, it had a few advantages. The pilot sat up high, with a good view over the nose which aided shooting at high deflection angles. Whereas in a high speed dive the ailerons of the Zero stiffened, becoming almost immoveable above 290mph (467km/hr), the Wildcat retained its effectiveness in the

US NAVY: THE OVERHEAD ATTACK

Whereas most other air arms concentrated on the no-deflection shot from astern the USN practised shots at high defection angles. The overhead attack, launched from a position almost directly above, was one. Attacks from high on the beam were also favored.

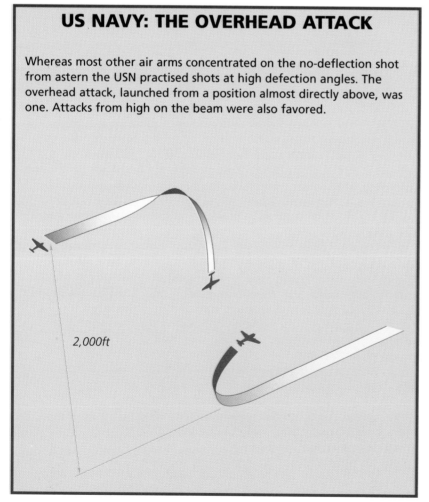

2,000ft

the fleet carriers *Shokaku* and *Zuikaku* were detached to support the light carrier *Shoho*, which was already in the area. They were opposed by the *Yorktown* and *Lexington*.

The battle was a comedy of errors. *Shoho* was sunk before noon on May 7; at the same time an American destroyer and oiler had been misidentified as a cruiser and a carrier, both of which were sunk by airplanes from the Japanese fleet carriers.

Low cloud and rain made visibility poor; the returning Japanese strike was engaged by a patrol of Wildcats, became confused, and two groups actually tried to line up and land on *Yorktown*. Unfortunately the Americans, understandably nervous about allowing Japanese bombers anywhere near them, did not allow them to do so!

On the following morning the opposing carrier forces located each other, and launched air strikes. Fighter defense on both sides was faulty. *Shokaku* was hit by two bombs and badly damaged. Both American carriers were hit. *Lexington* was lost some hours later due to faulty damage control, while *Yorktown* was damaged by a single bomb.

The Coral Sea battle can be accounted an honorable draw. It was also a learning time for the American Wildcat pilots. Shaken by being outmaneuvered by the Japanese airplanes, not only the Zeros but the dive- and torpedo bombers also, they endeavored to find tactical

answers to redress the balance.

The US Navy pilots had learned a great deal from RAF pilots sent to the USA to exchange ideas. They had already adopted the pair as the basic fighter element and, unlike virtually every other air arm in the world, had developed attacks which involved deflection shooting.

Jimmy Thach, commanding the Wildcats of VF-3, considered tactics which made the most of the relative survivability of their fighters vis-a-vis their opponents. The answer was the head-on

A Grumman Wildcat prepares to take off. The wooden flight deck typical of both American and Japanese carriers is clearly visible. A bomb would penetrate this with ease and explode in the hangar deck below.

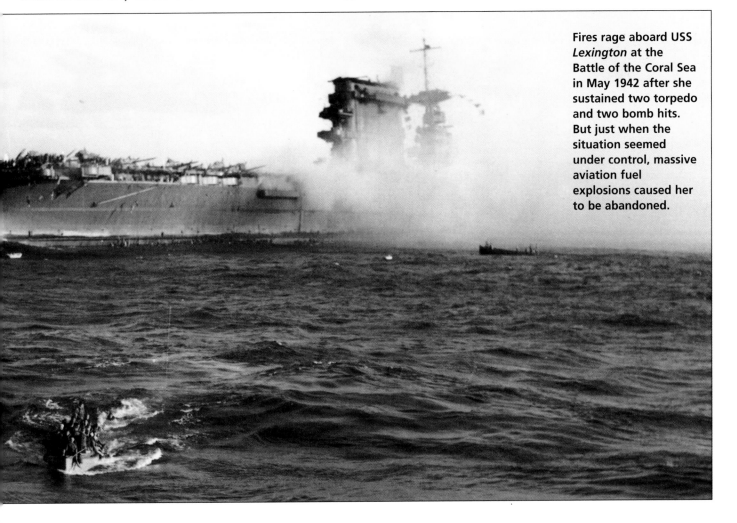

Fires rage aboard USS *Lexington* at the Battle of the Coral Sea in May 1942 after she sustained two torpedo and two bomb hits. But just when the situation seemed under control, massive aviation fuel explosions caused her to be abandoned.

attack, in which each fighter had an identical shot, and in which, if each pilot aimed accurately, the advantage went to the most survivable airplane. He came up with the Beam Defense Maneuver. A section of four fighters flew in two pairs abreast, with spacings related to minimum radius of turn at the current speed. Attacked from astern, one pair turned hard towards the other. On seeing this, the other pair turned hard towards the attacked section, passing below them. If the attacker had followed his prey around, he would end in a head-on pass with the other section, with the disadvantage of having to drop his nose, thereby risking a head-on collision, in order to shoot back.

MIDWAY, THE TURNING POINT

Midway Island was well-named; 1,300 miles (2,092km) northwest of Oahu, it was strategically placed on the direct route to Japan. Admiral Yamamoto conceived a plan to occupy it in June 1942, as the first step in launching an assault on the Hawaiian Islands. Unfortunately for him, the Americans had broken the Japanese codes, and knew precisely what he intended.

Direct support of the Midway invasion fleet was provided by four Japanese carriers: *Akagi*, *Kaga*, *Soryu* and *Hiryu*, the fighter complement of which was 103 A6M2 Zeros. Opposing them were three American carriers: *Hornet*, *Enterprise*, and the hastily repaired *Yorktown*. The garrison of Midway itself included 21 Buffaloes and seven Wildcats of the US Marines.

The Japanese opened the ball on June 4 with a strike against Midway. Directed by radar, the defenders intercepted, but were badly cut up by the Zeros. Japanese losses totalled nine, but

Douglas Dauntless dive bombers over Midway Island. In the Battle of Midway, Japanese fighter defenses were drawn down to low level by waves of American torpedo bombers, leaving the Dauntlesses with an unopposed run. All four Japanese fleet carriers were sunk.

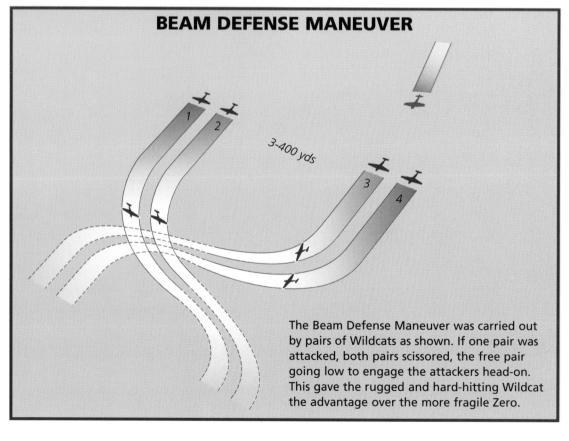

BEAM DEFENSE MANEUVER

3-400 yds

The Beam Defense Maneuver was carried out by pairs of Wildcats as shown. If one pair was attacked, both pairs scissored, the free pair going low to engage the attackers head-on. This gave the rugged and hard-hitting Wildcat the advantage over the more fragile Zero.

only five American fighters survived the initial attack in operable condition.

The riposte, from carrier- and Midway-based torpedo and dive bombers, was unco-ordinated, and the first attackers were cut to pieces for no result. Every aircraft of VT-8 was lost, mostly to Zeros, but the succession of attacks had drawn the defending Zeros down to low level. When Dauntless divebombers arrived over the Japanese fleet, they were unopposed, and in short order disposed of *Akagi*, *Kaga*, and *Soryu*.

Hiryu, the sole survivor, struck back. Her bombers penetrated the defensive fighter screen, albeit with heavy losses, seriously damaging Yorktown, which finally sank on June 7. *Enterprise* launched a counter-strike, and this scored four bomb hits on *Hiryu*, setting it ablaze. By morning of June 5, all four Japanese fleet carriers had sunk. Airplane losses during the battle, mainly due to fighters, were horrendous. Eighty-five American machines and the entire Japanese complement were destroyed, with the loss of many experienced and irreplaceable pilots. From this defeat the Imperial Japanese Navy air arm never recovered. Thach's Beam Defense Maneuver was first employed during this battle, which proved a turning point in the Pacific War. Thach himself became an ace at Midway; his total for the war was seven, and he became an Admiral.

GUADALCANAL

Two months after Midway, the USN took the offensive for the first time, when the Marines invaded Guadalcanal. Three carriers, *Enterprise*, *Saratoga* and *Wasp*, covered the landings with 99

Wildcats. The first Japanese counter-attack, of 27 twin-engined bombers escorted by 18 Zeros of the Tainan Air Group, which included Japanese aces Saburo Sakai and Hiroyoshi Nishizawa, was met in force, but nine Wildcats were shot down and several others badly damaged by the escorts, for four bombers and a Zero.

Desultory fighting ensued, with an average of slightly fewer than 20 fighter sorties per day. Over the next seven months, American fighter losses amounted to 79; 45 per 1,000 sorties, while the equivalent Japanese figures were 136; 73 per 1,000 sorties. By February 7 1943, Guadalcanal was firmly in American hands. Top-scoring Wildcat ace was US Marine Joe Foss, commonly known as "Swivel-Neck Joe", with 26 victories, thus equalling Eddie Rickenbacker's score in the Great War.

A Mitsubishi A6M5 Type 52 Zero-Sen hurtles down the deck of its carrier. The Zero was improved throughout the war, but was never able to match the performance of later American fighters.

Naval air power could intervene decisively in amphibious operations. Japanese transports at Guadalcanal burn, forming a backdrop to a Dauntless SBD on November 16 1942.

Whereas virtually all Japanese fighters had radial engines, the Kawasaki Ki-61 Hien was powered by a license-built Daimler-Benz DB 601. Operated by the Japanese Army, it was fast and agile, and armed with four 12.7mm machine guns.

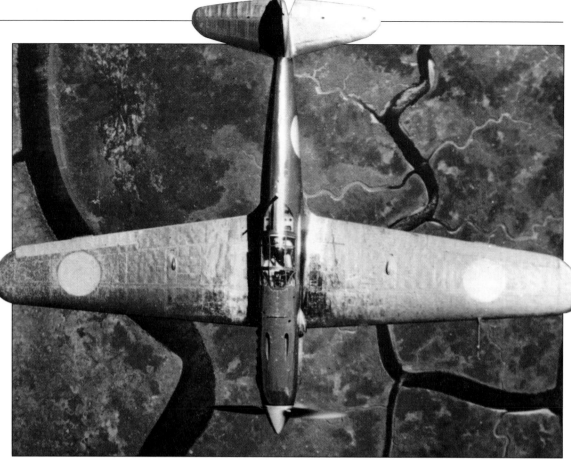

Foss was closely followed by John L Smith with 19 victories; Marion Carl with 15½, Robert Galer with 14; Eugene Trowbridge (13); Ken Frazier (12½); and Harold (Indian Joe) Bauer, who was killed on November 14 1943, his score 10.

Many top-scoring aces of the crack Tainan Kokutai of the Imperial Japanese Navy were lost during the Guadalcanal fighting. Notably these were Saburo Sakai (61 victories), who was withdrawn wounded, having lost an eye; Toshio Ohta (34); Junichi Sasai (27); Kazushi Uto (19); Toraichi Takatsuka (16); Shigetaka Ohmori (13); and Keisaku Yoshimura and Motosuna Yoshida (12 each), who were all killed. Ranking Japanese ace Hiroyoshi Nishizawa died shortly after, shot down as a passenger in a transport aircraft. The hastily recruited replacements were of such poor quality that the unit, like many others, became a shadow of its former self.

PACIFIC STRATEGY

Whilst the USN and USMC played a tremendous part in the Pacific War, they were not alone. The RAAF and RNZAF fought alongside them, albeit in small numbers, while the USAAF was present in strength.

The conduct of the Pacific War bred two schools of thought. The US Navy favored an island-hopping campaign via the Gilberts, bypassing the Marshalls to Eniwetok; then bypassing the Japanese base at Truk to advance upon the Japanese home islands. By contrast, the USAAF, tied to fixed land bases, preferred an advance from New Guinea to the Philippines, then on to Japan. In the event both were adopted.

While apparently wasteful of resources, this had one tremendous advantage. The Japanese, already badly overstretched, never knew where the next thrust was coming from, and consequently remained weak everywhere. All they could do was to react when the next blow fell, using their depleted forces as a fire brigade and rushing them from place to place.

The Americans made no attempt to drive back the Japanese in a linear manner. Instead, they frequently bypassed Japanese garrisons, cutting them off from supplies and reinforcements, to wither on the vine, having first neutralized their offensive capability, usually via air strikes. In this manner several Japanese enclaves were left

Flak bursts stain the sky as a Zero tries to penetrate the defenses of the US fleet in the Sulu Sea. It failed, and was shot down shortly after this picture was taken. Center is an American escort carrier.

CARRIER FIGHTER COMPARISONS, 1939-1945

Type	Speed (mph/km/hr)	Ceiling(ft/m)	Climb	Range(miles/km)
Blackburn Skua	225/362	19,100/5,821	1,580ft/min (8.02m/sec)	760/1,223
Grumman F4F-4 Wildcat	320/515	34,000/10,363	12min 24sec to 20,000ft (6,096m)	830/1,336
Brewster F2A Buffalo	321/517	33,200/10,119	2,290ft/min (11.63m/sec)	965/1,553
Fairey Fulmar I	256/412	22,400/7,349	1,105ft/min (5.61m/sec)	830/1,336
Mitsubishi A6M6c Zero-Sen	346/557	35,100/10,698	7min 56sec to 20,000ft (6,096m)	1,130/1,818
Fairey Firefly	316/508	28,000/8,534	5min 45sec to 10,000ft (3,048m)	1,300/2,092

on New Guinea, which is a huge island, while among others the Marshall Islands were bypassed in a leap to Eniwetok, as was the large naval base at Truk.

Some idea of American numerical superiority combined with changing technical superiority can be given by the statistics. The campaign for Eastern New Guinea between February 1 and August 31 1942 saw 1,900 Allied fighter sorties flown, against about 1,000 Japanese. Allied fighter losses amounted to 177; Japanese fighter losses totaled just 41; an adverse ratio of 4.32:1. The campaign for New Guinea and New Britain, between September 15 1942 and June 30 1943, yielded 8,600 Allied fighter sorties against about 4,000 by the Japanese, with losses of 114 and 380 respectively; a positive ratio of 1:3.33. The fighting over Rabaul which followed between October 1 1943 and February 17 1944 was marked by 5,345 Allied fighter sorties against about 2,400 Japanese; losses were 112 Allied fighters against 330 Japanese; a positive ratio of 1:2.95.

In all cases, the Allies flew roughly two fighter sorties to each Japanese one, whereas the victory/loss ratio switched from extremely adverse to very positive. This actually reflects

A Nakajima B5N torpedo bomber threads its way past two US Navy cruisers and heads for an American carrier at the Battle of Santa Cruz on October 26 1942. The air defense fighters have failed to stop it; it is now down to the ship's guns.

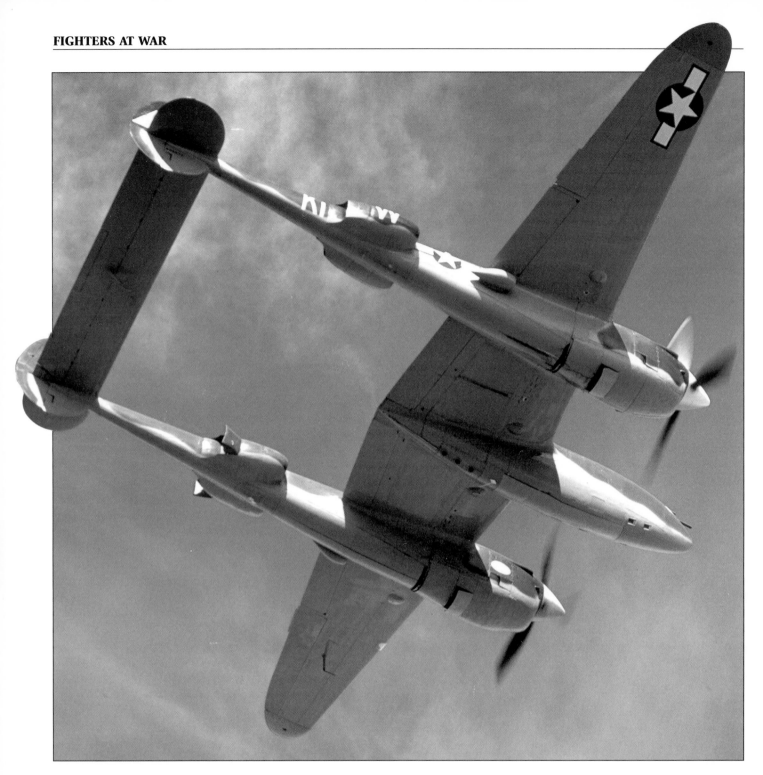

The bulges on the twin booms indicate the location of the turbo-chargers, which gave the Lockheed P-38 Lightning its exceptional high-speed, high-altitude performance. Its long range was well-suited to the island-hopping war conducted by the USAAF.

three factors. Firstly, the introduction of American fighters which were superior to their Japanese counterparts. Secondly, the effect of superior training and teamwork, which allowed the numerical superiority to afford more coincidental support. Thirdly, the Japanese fighter arm, both army and navy, had lost many experienced pilots by the end of 1943. This even allowed Wildcats, which flew from the smaller escort carriers for the remainder of the war, to hold their own.

THE USAAF IN THE PACIFIC

At the outbreak of the war against Japan, the two main USAAF fighter types were the Curtiss P-40, which we examined earlier, and the Bell P-39 Airacobra.

The Airacobra was unconventional in that its engine, the Allison V-1710, was mounted amidships, behind the pilot, and drove the propeller by means of a long and weighty transmission shaft. This arrangement promised several advantages. The cockpit could be located forward, improving the view over the nose. Placing the engine on the centre of gravity should have improved maneuvrability, while this configuration allowed a nosewheel undercarriage, with superior ground handling and view on takeoff.

Alas the Airacobra proved a turkey. The unorthodox engine location resulted in extreme weight penalties; in an already underpowered fighter this proved disastrous, and it was easily outfought by the Zero and Hayabusa. The unreliability of the Allison was compounded by poor access for routine maintenance; the result was chronic unserviceability.

By far the most successful USAAF fighter in

China and the Pacific was Lockheed's P-38 Lightning, which largely supplanted the P-40 Warhawk from mid-1943. Its exceptional range made it ideal for the long-distance missions which were standard in the Pacific, while its speed and altitude performance gave it a distinct edge over most Japanese fighters that it encountered. Its high wing loading meant that it was unable to turn with them but, by staying high and choosing their moment, Lightning pilots were able to succeed against their better-turning adversaries by using dive and zoom tactics.

Both top-scoring American pilots of the war, Dick Bong (40) and Tommy McGuire (38), achieved most of their victories with the Lightning. Bong survived the war only to die shortly after in a takeoff accident with the P-80 Shooting Star jet. McGuire died in action while trying to save a fellow pilot under attack; he attempted a too-tight turn just above the tree-tops but stalled and went in.

OFFENSIVE IN THE PACIFIC

The Grumman Aircraft Corporation has traditionally been known as "The Ironworks", its airplanes being so rugged that rumor had it that they were carved out of the solid. Even before America's entry into the war, it was obvious that the performance of the Wildcat was inferior to that of land-based fighters in Europe. Chance Vought's Corsair was undergoing trials as a potential Wildcat

replacement, but in a "belt and braces" decision, the US Navy went to Grumman for an upgraded Wildcat.

The result, first flown on June 26 1942, was the F6F Hellcat. Powered by a Wright Double Wasp 18-cylinder radial engine, the Hellcat retained the simple lines of its predecessor, and although considerably larger and heavier was much faster, climbed better, and out-turned it with ease. From its combat debut in August 1943, the Hellcat comfortably out-performed

The Allison-engined P-51 Mustang, also known as the A-36 in its close air support incarnation, gave first-class service against the Japanese in Burma and China. In these theaters it did not need high-altitude capability.

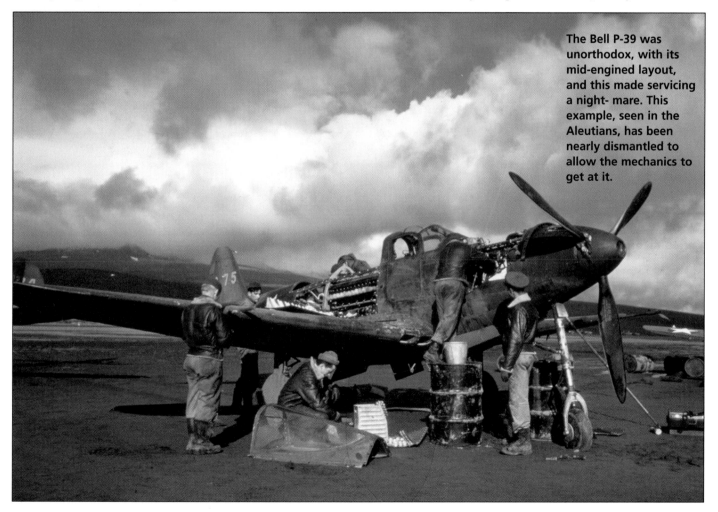

The Bell P-39 was unorthodox, with its mid-engined layout, and this made servicing a night-mare. This example, seen in the Aleutians, has been nearly dismantled to allow the mechanics to get at it.

CHANCE VOUGHT F4U-4 CORSAIR

Dimensions: Span 41ft (12.50m); Length 33ft 8in (10.26m); Height 14ft 9in (4.50m); Wing area 314sq.ft (29.17m²).
Power: One Pratt & Whitney R-2800-18W 18-cylinder air-cooled radial engine rated at 2,100hp.
Weights: Empty 9,205lb (4,175kg); Loaded 14,670lb (6,654kg).
Performance: Maximum speed 446mph (718km/hr); Ceiling 41,500ft (12,649m); Climb 7min 42sec to 20,000ft (6,096m); Range 1,005 miles (1,617km).
Armament: Six wing-mounted .50in(12.7mm) Browning machine guns with 2,350 rounds total.

The first American fighter able to exceed 400mph(644km/hr), the Corsair owed its success to its overwhelming performance. It was designed as the smallest possible airframe wrapped around the largest possible engine, although this involved a very poor view from the cockpit. Intended as a carrier fighter, tricky handling coupled with a bad bounce while deck-landing ensured that it made its combat debut with the US Marine Corps, operating from land bases. The cockpit was later raised and the bounce cured; once this was done the Corsair became a very successful naval fighter, in service with many nations, which did not cease production until 1952, long after all its contemporaries.

the Zero, and gave the US Navy a measure of air superiority over the next two years. British Corsair pilot Norman Hanson tried the Hellcat for a local flight on one occasion. He commented afterwards:

"In landing particularly I found it a lot safer and easier to handle largely, I think, because of its superior visibility and better stall characteristics."

Even before the requirement that led to the Hellcat, another fighter powered by the Double Wasp was under development for the USN. This was the Chance Vought F4U Corsair. To make the most of the available power, a huge four-bladed propeller was needed. This caused problems with ground clearance, to solve which an inverted gull-wing configuration was adopted. The resultant bird became known as "The bent-wing bastard from Stratford, Illinois."

One of the fastest fighters of the war, the Corsair was less than ideal for carrier operations. It had the endurance; it had the speed; it had the hitting power; but forward

The deck-landing characteristics of the Corsair were poor, and the first service to use it as a carrier fighter was the Royal Navy, from April 1944. The USMC used it from land bases from February 1943, and top-scoring Marine Greg Boyington gained most of his victories with it.

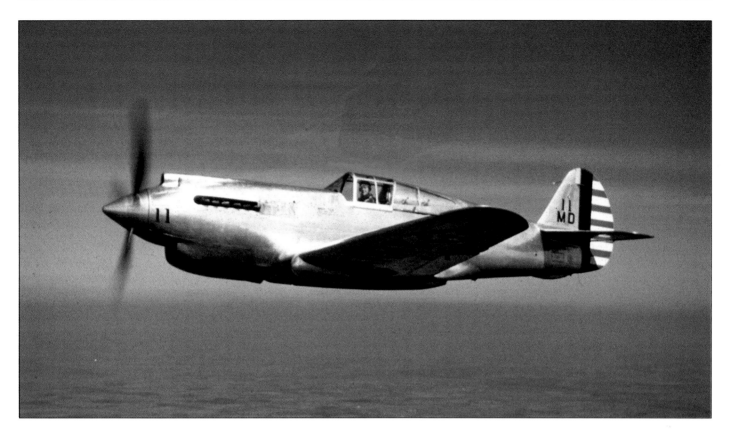

view from the cockpit, so important in a carrier-based airplane, was appalling; while for deck landing it had a built-in bounce which compromised safety. British Fleet Air Arm pilot Norman Hanson's reaction on first seeing it was to go and make his will!

The Corsair was originally judged unsuitable for carrier operations, and issued instead to the Marines. Combat debut was made on February 13 1943 over Guadalcanal, and within six months all USMC Squadrons had re-equipped with the Corsair, the blinding performance of which completely outclassed its opponents. While much heavier wing-loaded than the Zero, it could generally stay with it for the first 90 degrees of turn, and this was usually enough. Not for nothing did it earn the name of "The Whistling Death!" from the Japanese.

It was in fact left to the Royal Navy to operate the Corsair from carriers, which they did from April 1944; nine months earlier than the US Navy. It was certainly a fact that more Corsairs were lost as a result of landing accidents than ever fell to Japanese fighters. But FAA Corsairs had the wings clipped to fit below decks, and surprisingly this cured the floating that occurred over the deck due to ground effect. Another innovation was a small spoiler under the starboard wing, which ensured that at the stall that wing always dropped first. But when, at the end of 1944, the British Pacific Fleet, with Corsairs, Hellcats, Fireflies and Seafires, joined the Americans in the assault on Japan, opportunities for air combat were few, and there were virtually no aces in their ranks.

Meanwhile Marine Corps Corsairs operated the type with great success from island bases. The top-scoring Marine pilot of the war was Gregory Boyington, with 28 victories. The antithesis of the clean-cut, milk-drinking and early-to-bed all-American boy, Boyington was a hard-living, whiskey-drinking hell-raiser. Having prejudiced his career by a tangled private life, he joined the Flying Tigers, the American Volunteer Group in south-east Asia.

Flying P-40s from Rangoon in Burma, he downed six Japanese aircraft in four weeks, before returning to the USA. On his return to the USA, he rejoined the Marines, and in September 1943 was in command of VMF-214, the Black Sheep squadron.

Tactical finesse was no part of Boyington's makeup; on his first mission, on September 16, the Black Sheep blundered into about 40 Zeros, and an unholy dogfight resulted. When Boyington returned, he claimed five Zeros. One of the fightingest men ever to strap an airplane on his back, he sought every opportunity to bring the Japanese to battle, and by Christmas of that year had reached the American record of

The Curtiss P-40 was the most numerous USAAF type in the early years of the Pacific War, and although largely supplanted by the P-38, remained in service until the end. The final variant was the P-40N Warhawk.

The Supermarine Seafire was the carrier variant of the immortal Spitfire. Although an excellent fighter, it was too short-ranged and not strong enough for carrier work.

26 victories, held jointly by Eddie Rickenbacker in the Great War, and Marine pilot Joe Foss. On January 3 1944 he got two more, but was himself shot down while attempting to protect his stricken wingman. He survived a low-level bale-out by a miracle, to end the war in a Japanese prison camp.

THE MARIANAS TURKEY SHOOT

By the middle of 1944, the Japanese were being driven back on all fronts. Overmatched, the Japanese carriers had avoided battle for the past year, but now it had become do or die. When in June 1944 the American Pacific fleet sallied forth against the Marianas, bypassing Truk and the Caroline Islands, the Japanese were forced to act.

The American Task Force contained seven fleet carriers and eight light carriers, with two groups of escort carriers to provide close air support. Total fighter strength was 470 F6F-3 Hellcats. Against this armada, the Japanese could bring nine carriers, reinforced by many more land-based aircraft.

The Japanese plan was to catch the American Task Force between the anvil of land-based air power and the hammer of carrier aircraft. As the poet said, the best laid plans. . . . Poor intelligence, operational inadequacies, and a determined foe added up to utter disaster for the Japanese.

On June 11 over 200 Hellcats carried out a sweep over Japanese airfields in the Marianas. On the following day, heavy raids were launched against Saipan, Tinian and Guam. That evening, part of the force raced north to attack Iwo Jima and Chichi Jima. Its task complete, it rejoined two days later. By now the anvil had been irreparably shattered.

Grumman Hellcats patrol over Rutavitari Island, Kiribati, after a bombing raid on the oil facility at King's Wharf, from where smoke is rising.

GRUMMAN F6F-3 HELLCAT

Dimensions: Span 42ft 10in (13.06m);
Length 33ft 7in (10.23m); Height 11ft 3in (3.43m);
Wing area 334sq.ft (31.03m²).
Power: One Pratt & Whitney R-2800 Double Wasp 18-cylinder air-cooled radial engine rated at 2,000hp.
Weights: Empty 9,042lb (4,101kg);
Loaded 12,186lb (5,528kg).
Performance: Maximum speed 376mph (605km/hr);
Ceiling 37,500ft (11,429m); Climb 14min to 25,000ft
(7,620m); Range 1,085 miles (1,746km).
Armament: Six wing-mounted .50in (12.7mm) Colt-Browning machine guns with 400 rpg.

The most important ship-board fighter of the war, the Hellcat made its combat debut on August 31 1943. It was faster than the Japanese Zero, although it could not climb at such a steep angle, and was exceptionally well-protected against enemy fire. With 456lb (207kg) of armor plating, bullet-proof glass, duralumin deflector plates and self-sealing for the fuel tanks, it could absorb an enormous amount of battle damage and still function. Flown by former Wildcat pilots who had learned the hard way to offset the superior maneuvrability of the Zero through teamwork and tactics, it immediately established an ascendancy over the Japanese fighter; an ascendancy that it never lost throughout the war.

This left only the hammer. Belatedly, the Japanese fleet sailed on June 13, and was immediately reported by US submarines. Unaware that the anvil no longer existed, Admiral Ozawa divided his force into two parts. The first was bait to draw the American carriers within range of the second, killer group.

The carrier battle commenced on June 19, when the first Japanese strike was launched. Detected by radar at the extreme range of 150 miles (241km), defending Hellcats were scrambled to meet them. An unexpected bonus was that the Japanese paused to orbit 75 miles (120km) away while the strike leader briefed his inexperienced crews by radio. This hiatus enabled the American fighters to intercept far out from the Task Force, with all the advantages of height and position. The ensuing engagement was more a massacre than a battle.

Wave after wave of Japanese aircraft set out for the American carrier force, but were met by wave after wave of defending Hellcats, which wrought tremendous destruction. Japanese losses during the day amounted to 218, and only a few attackers broke through the defenses, causing minimal damage.

American submarines now played their part. They torpedoed and sank the carriers *Taiho* and *Shokaku*. On the following day the American carriers went over to the offensive, sinking *Hiyo* and damaging *Zuikaku* and *Chiyoda*. US Navy losses to all causes amounted to 130 airplanes and 76 aircrewmen. Total Japanese losses, including land-based airplanes, were 476, including about 445 aircrewmen. The Imperial Japanese Navy never recovered from this setback. The last great carrier battle of the war, it had been a great American victory, thanks

mainly to the prowess of the Hellcat pilots.

Aloft during the Marianas battle was top-scoring US Navy pilot David McCampbell. An "old man" of 34 at the time, he was Carrier Air Group Commander aboard the USS *Essex*, and his first victory was scored over Saipan on June 11. Then on June 19 he led a flight of 14 Hellcats to intercept a Japanese raid near Guam, claiming five Yokosuka D4Y divebombers during the one

An Aichi D3A dive bomber sets off on a sortie. One of the last machines in service with a fixed undercarriage, it was very maneuvrable, which often enabled it to evade Allied fighters.

Japanese torpedos were the most deadly of any nation. Here a three-seater Nakajima B5N speeds down the deck with its deadly cargo, but as this picture is dated January 5 1945, it stands almost no chance of completing its mission.

Operating from bases on Iwo Jima, P-51D Mustangs of the USAAF flew eight-hour escort missions, the longest of the war, to protect B-29 heavy bombers. This is an early production model.

sortie. Later that day, over Guam, he claimed two more. But at the end of that trip he was outmaneuvered by a Zero flown by one of the few remaining Japanese honchos, and forced to disengage with a high speed dive. Other Hellcats intervened, and brushed the Zero off his tail.

McCampbell's biggest day came on October 23 1944, when he and his wingman Roy Rushing encountered about 40 Japanese Zeros escorting a bomber raid. While others tackled the bombers, McCampbell and Rushing set about the fighters. The latter were not very aggressive and appeared to be totally

inexperienced, and allowed the two Hellcats to attack as and when they chose. At the end of the engagement McCampbell claimed nine and Rushing five. McCampbell survived the war with a score of 34 victories.

THE ASSAULT ON JAPAN

Gradually the Japanese had abandoned their doctrine of light and maneuvrable, but extremely vulnerable, fighters, in exchange for more heavily armed and protected airplanes. Of these, the Ki-61 Hien was unusual in that it was powered by a liquid-cooled V-12 engine. The Ki-

One of the best Japanese fighters of the late war period was the Nakajima Ki-84 Hayate. Very fast, and difficult to intercept, what it lacked was experienced pilots to exploit its full potential.

JAPANESE LAND-BASED FIGHTERS, 1941-1945

Type	Speed (mph/km/hr)	Ceiling (ft/m)	Climb	Range miles/km
Nakajima Ki-43 Hayabusa	320/515	36,747/11,200	5min 49sec to 16,405ft (5,000m)	1,006/1,619
Nakajima Ki-44 Shoki	376/605	35,435/10,800	4min 26sec to 16,405ft (5,000m)	980/1,577
Kawasaki Ki-61 Hien	348/560	32,810/10,000	7min to 16,405ft (5,000m)	1,119/1,800
Mitsubishi J2M3 Raiden	363/584	36,091/11,000	3,838ft/min (19.50m/sec)	655/1,055
Nakajima Ki-84 Hayate	388/624	34,450/10,500	11min 40sec to 26,248ft (8,000m)	1,025/1,650

KAWANISHI N1K2-J SHIDEN-KAI

Dimensions: Span 39ft 3¼in (11.98m);
Length 30ft 8in (9.35m); Height 13ft (3.96m);
Wing area 253sq.ft (23.50m²).
Power: One Nakajima NK9H Homare 21 18-cylinder
air-cooled radial engine rated at 1,990hp.
Weights: Empty 5,858lb (2,657kg);
Loaded 9,039lb (4,100kg).
Performance: Maximum speed 370mph (595km/hr);
Ceiling 35,300ft (60m); Climb 7min 22sec to 19,685ft
(6,000m); Range 1,069 miles (1,720km).
Armament: Four wing-mounted 20mm Type 99
cannon.

With the service entry of the Hellcat and Corsair, Japan urgently needed a high-performance interceptor. New fighters were under development, but this took time. Readily available was the Kyofu, a floatplane fighter with a mid-wing configuration and, like the American Mustang, a low-drag laminar-flow aerofoil. This was rapidly developed into the Shiden. Maneuvrability was increased using a unique combat flap system which changed angle automatically to provide extra lift during high-g maneuvers. While it was as fast as the Hellcat, and climbed and turned much better, the Shiden was tricky to fly, and only an experienced pilot could get the best out of it.

43 Shoki was relatively highly wing loaded, while the performances of the J2M3 Raiden and the Ki-84 Hayate were good by any standards. The best Japanese Navy fighter of the war was however the NiK2 Shiden, which in the hands of an experienced pilot had the mastery over the Hellcat. But with all these, the story was too little, too late.

B-29 heavy bombers commenced raiding the Japanese home islands from the Marianas on November 24 1944. Lack of effective early warning and airborne radar meant that defending Japanese fighters were hard-pressed to intercept. Aircraft factories and airfields were high on the list of targets, and Japanese fighter production fell alarmingly.

Daylight bombing began in March 1945, once fighter escort became available. This was provided by Mustangs based on Iwo Jima, flying the longest (eight hour) escort missions on record. Mustangs over Tokyo signalled the beginning of the end for the Japanese. In July 1945, the US Navy joined the assault on Japan, with 14 or more aircraft carriers at a time, supplemented by the British Pacific Fleet, and able to put more than 1,000 airplanes into the air at one time.

Heavily outnumbered, the Japanese defenders fought back with the strength of desperation, but unavailingly. The final British air combat of the war took place on August 12, when ten Seafires accounted for eight Zeros, losing one of their own number. The final victory of the war fell to a USN Corsair, which shot down a C6N Saiun, only minutes before the end of hostilities.

One of the most difficult interception problems in the Pacific was the rocket-propelled Yokosuka Okha *kamikaze* aircraft. Dropped from a bomber many miles from the fleet, it swept in at over 500mph (800km/hr).

Faster and Higher

1946-1958

Reconnaissance was vital if bomb raids were to be effective. The largest bomber ever to enter service, the Convair RB-36D, carries an RF-84F Thunderflash beneath its belly. On nearing the target, the RF-84F detaches itself, flies the mission, and then returns to mother.

The first MiG-15 to fall into American hands was this one, flown in by Ro Kun Suk, a North Korean defector. This picture has been crudely censored; while the red star on the fin has been air-brushed out, the star on the fuselage remains.

A TRUISM of both world wars was that he who has height controls the battle. Height depended largely on available power, and by 1946 piston-engined fighters had reached the limits of their practical development. The future was the jet engine.

The first jet engines used compressors of two types, centrifugal flow and axial flow. The first was primarily developed by the British, who drew extensively on their vast experience of the design of two-stage superchargers. The first German jets were axial flow, and while this configuration eventually superseded the centrifugal compressor, it was for a long time inferior to it.

The quest for greater performance continued. One of the main problems to be overcome was compressibility. As speeds increased, the air ahead of the airplane was unable to move out of the way fast enough, and became compressed. As an airplane is an uneven shape, so the compression was also uneven, which gave rise to severe buffeting, adversely affecting handling, which worsened as the speed of sound was approached.

The speed of sound varies with air density, which depends on altitude and temperature. For most practical purposes it is 761mph (1,225km/hr) at sea level, falling to 660mph (1,062km/hr) at 36,090ft (11,000m), above which it remains constant. To overcome problems caused by this variation, it is measured in terms of the Mach number, the speed of sound being Mach 1.0. Compressibility could be minimized by using relatively thin wings, measured in terms of thickness/chord ratio.

Aerodynamic drag rises in proportion to the square of the speed. Therefore if speed doubles, drag quadruples. It was however found that if

The Lockheed F-80 Shooting Star was the first USAF jet fighter. Straight-winged, it was outperformed by the swept-winged MiG-15 and, despite an occasional success, spent most of the war in the close air support role.

the wing was raked back at an angle, the velocity of the airflow was effectively reduced in proportion to the cosine of the sweep angle. Once this was accepted, most high-performance airplanes featured swept-back wings.

WAR OVER KOREA

In fighter combat, the ever higher trend reached its peak in the Korean War. The country had been partitioned at the end of World War II, and subsequent attempts to unify it had failed. Then in June 1950 communist North Korea attempted to settle the matter by force of arms.

Opposed by the Far Eastern Air Force of the USAF, the small and obsolete North Korean Air Force was swept from the sky, and the American fighters turned their attention to close air support. The ground campaign was successful, and by November United Nations troops had

advanced almost to the border of the People's Republic of China.

At this point the Chinese joined the war in overwhelming numbers and thrust the UN forces back. At the same time, Russian swept-wing jet fighters rose from bases inside China to join the fray. For many years it was either not known, or not admitted in the West, that most of the MiG-15 pilots who flew in Korea were actually Russians. When one considers that the MiG-15 had only begun to equip Soviet units during the winter of 1949-50, this seems obvious; it is hard to imagine them handing over large numbers to the Chinese and North Koreans at this stage!

The first jet versus jet combat in history took place on November 8, when Russell Brown, flying an F-80C Shooting Star of the 51st Fighter Interceptor Wing, shot down a MiG. On the

For servicing, the Grumman F9F Panther came apart like a Meccano set. On one occasion a gray Marine Corps Panther was fitted with a dark blue Navy tail, to become "The Blue-tailed Fly!". Conversely a Navy jet received a gray tail to become "Vice Versa"!

HMS *Glory* seen on station in Korean waters with Sea Furies ranged on deck. Outperformed by the MiG-15, the Sea Fury was far more maneuvrable, and on August 9 1952 Sea Furies from HMS *Ocean* shot down two MiGs.

following day, US Navy pilot Bill Amen, flying an F9F Panther of VF-111, downed another.

In each case the MiG pilots had made a tactical mistake and bled off speed in front of the American airplanes. This was not often repeated; the MiG-15 was far faster, and had a much better altitude performance than the straight-winged American fighters. Boeing B-29s, which had been bombing the north in relative safety, soon proved vulnerable, and the escorting F-80s were unable to give them adequate protection. The USAF sent for their latest fighter, the F-86 Saber, as a matter of urgency. A handful of Sabers arrived in mid-December 1950; were operational within days, and encountered the MiG-15 for the first time on December 17. Ahead lay almost 31 months of incessant fighting, in a battle for air superiority which became legendary.

First flown on December 30 1947, the MiG-15 was designed as a bomber destroyer. A simple, no frills fighter, the MiG-15bis variant could reach 32,810ft (10,000m) in 4 minutes 54 seconds, and had a service ceiling of 50,856ft (15,500m), both exceptional for the time. It was stressed to a load factor of 8g, and was exceptionally heavily armed with one 37mm and two 23mm cannon mounted in the nose. Russian experts calculated that an average of just two hits by 37mm, or eight hits by 23mm shells, would be enough to destroy even a B-29. As they had reverse-engineered confiscated B-29s and produced them as the Tu-4, they were not working entirely from theory!

Against fighters this armament was less than satisfactory. A single hit was likely to be devastating, but the difficulty was in obtaining hits. The rate of fire of these large cannon was slow, and ammunition supply small, 40 rounds at roughly seven per second for the 37mm, and 80 rounds each at 14 rounds per second for the 23mm cannon, giving less than six seconds of firing time. The ballistic qualities and trajectories of each caliber differed widely. In practice this meant that it was virtually impossible to harmonize the guns on a point; some American fighter pilots have described being shot at, with the light 23mm shells passing over them while the heavy 37mm shells went under! Long on tradition, the USAF instituted the "Six O'Clock Club" for those who had survived a MiG attack!

The airframe of the MiG-15 was fairly basic. The 35 degree swept wings had two fences each to inhibit spanwise flow, and the high-set tail was swept at the same angle. Finish was the usual Soviet-standard crude but good enough. What really made the difference was the engine.

The Korean War gave the Mustang a new lease of life. Its load-carrying capability and long endurance, combined with its agility, made it far more suitable for close air support than the short-legged jets.

JET FIGHTERS OF THE KOREAN WAR, PERFORMANCE

Type	Speed (mph-km/hr)	Ceiling (ft/m)	Climb	Range (miles/km)
Lockheed F-80 Shooting Star	580/933	39,500/12,039	5min 30sec to 20,000ft/6,096m	780/1,255
Republic F-84 Thunderjet	598/962	40,750/12,420	5,800ft/min (29.46m/sec)	805/1,295
Gloster Meteor F.8	590/949	44,000/13,411	6,950ft/min (35.30m/sec)	980/1,577
North American F-86F Saber	678/1,091	48,000/14,630	8,100ft/min (41.15m/sec)	926/1,490
Mikoyan & Gurevitch MiG-15bis	688/1,107	50,856/15,500	4min 54sec to 32,810ft (10,000m)	702/1,130
Grumman F9F Panther	579/932	42,800/13,045	5,090ft/min (25.86m/sec)	1,300/2,092

The MiG-17 was a derivative of the MiG-15, with slightly different wing planform, and afterburners. It and its predecessor were built in enormous numbers, probably exceeding that of any other jet, and exported to more than 40 countries (Czech Air Force machine shown here), although the MiG-17 was too late to have seen service in the Korean War.

The Soviet Union had signally failed to develop a suitable engine. They were saved by the idiocy of the British government of the day, which in 1947 sold them Rolls-Royce Derwent and Nene engines. The Nene was at that time probably the best jet engine in the world.

It was quickly copied, and incorporated into the MiG-15, with the addition of water injection, as the Klimov RD-45F. It was then further developed into the VK-1 for the MiG-15bis, which provided 5,952lb (2,700kg) of static thrust. This was comparable to the power of the General Electric engines of the later F-86 variants, with the difference that the normal loaded weight of the airframe that they had to push around the sky was much less than that of the American fighter. And it was a combination of better thrust/weight ratio, and the superior high-altitude performance of its engine, which allowed the MiG-15 to outperform the Saber in all respects except maximum speed.

The first flight of the North American F-86 Saber predated that of the MiG-15 by three months. Like the Russian fighter, it had a nose inlet and swept wings, although the horizontal tail surfaces were mounted rather lower. Power was supplied by the General Electric J47 axial-flow turbojet, and it was armed with six fast-firing .50 caliber Colt-Brownings, with 267 rounds per gun, giving over 13 seconds of firing time.

The MiG-15bis acquired by the USAF was subjected to intensive flight and evaluation trials in Japan. Later it was flown to Wright-Patterson AB in the USA, where it is seen in USAF markings. It is now in the USAF Museum.

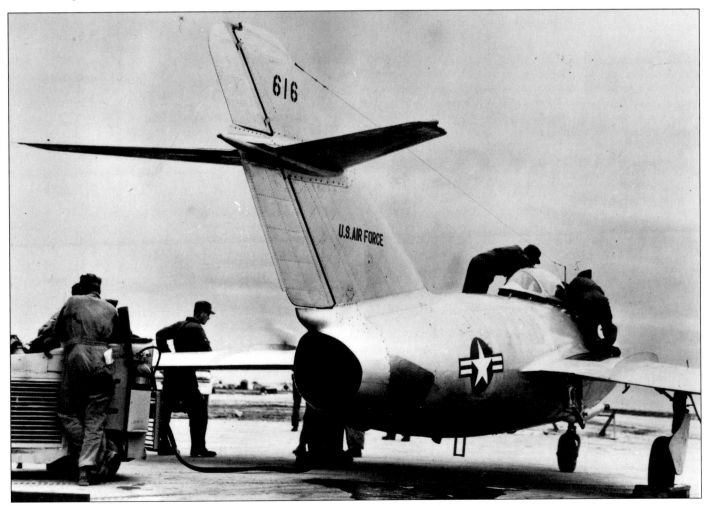

Overall the Saber was considerably larger and heavier, while its systems were considerably more sophisticated. Whereas the MiG carried a simple gyro gunsight, that of the Saber had radar ranging, a considerable asset in combat. American flight control systems were also superior.

MIG ALLEY

The first victory of one swept wing jet fighter over another came on December 17 1950, when Saber driver Bruce Hinton downed a MiG-15. It was the first of hundreds. At the armistice in July 1953, USAF Sabers claimed a victory/loss ratio of 14:1, but this was officially amended to 7½:1, the actual figures being 757 victories to 103 losses. Unsurprisingly, the Russians deny this, claiming 1,097 UN airplanes shot down (651 of them Sabers) for 335 losses. They also claim that their Chinese and North Korean allies accounted for 271 UN airplanes, (181 Sabers) for 231 losses.

Communist fighter pilots claimed more than eight Sabers for each one actually lost. Of course, the high altitudes where much of the action took place often made it all but impossible for a victorious pilot to see his victim hit the ground, but as the vast majority of Saber losses came down in communist territory, a search on the ground should have quickly established the accuracy of many claims.

Overclaiming is an enduring feature of air combat, and in the stress and confusion of battle is quite understandable. But admitted communist air combat losses total 566. If these figures are not

The F-86 Saber was flown in Korea by Australian and South African squadrons as well as by the USAF. It was later adopted by many other air arms. These are Canadair Saber 4s of 112 Squadron RAAF.

The clean lines of the Saber with its swept wings and tail are clearly seen here. It was developed through many sub-types, including the Fury carrier fighter for the US Navy.

rigged, and there seems little reason to assume that they are not at least in the right field, Saber pilots claimed 1.33 MiGs for each MiG lost.

Compared with overclaiming levels in previous campaigns, this reflects extremely creditably on the standards by which their victories were awarded. It also confirms what has long been known; that the Saber pilots were victorious in Korea. All that differs is the victory/loss ratio, which becomes 5½:1 rather than the 7½:1 ratified in September 1970 by the official Saber Measures (Charlie) study.

Another factor is the circumstances under which the two swept-wing fighter types fought. UN fighter-bombers roamed the north at medium and low altitudes, carrying out interdiction and close air support missions vital to the success of the ground war. Had the MiGs been allowed to harry them uninterrupted, the entire campaign would have been jeopardized. The task of the Sabers was to contain the MiGs. This they did by ranging north right to the Chinese border at high altitude, in position to intercept the Russian fighters if they attempted to slip past below to attack the fighter-bombers.

This forced the communists to react by seeking an altitude advantage over the Sabers in their turn, making to a great extent the fighter war a separate conflict, fought between five and eight miles (8-13km) above the ground, and effectively divorced from it.

In doing so the Sabers were considerably handicapped. They had to fly upwards of 200 miles (322km) to MiG Alley, far beyond the reach of allied radar cover. Once there, they had to patrol, possibly fight against odds, and then return. Even with drop tanks this stretched their endurance to the limit.

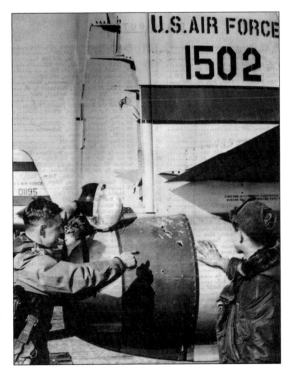

The other American straight-winged fighter in Korea was the F-84 Thunderjet. John Glina examines damage caused to his jet by communist ground fire. When hit, the impact lifted his feet off the rudder pedals.

107

An F-86E drops its tanks over Korea. The aircraft in the background is Elenore E, which claimed 9½ MiGs over Korea. Second War ace William Whisner got five in this airplane to add to his 15½ Germans over Europe.

For most of the Korean War Russians flew the MiG-15, but it is believed that Warsaw Pact pilots also participated. This lineup is of Polish aircraft. The MiG-15 was designed as a bomber destroyer; it was less good against fighters.

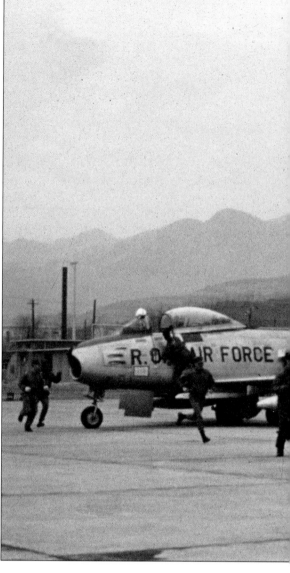

It would have helped if the MiG airfields could have been attacked, but these were in China, and off limits. UN airplanes were forbidden even to cross the border, which gave the MiGs a sanctuary in which they could take off and gain altitude before crossing into North Korea. It also gave them a haven into which they could retire when the going got rough, although once combat had been joined, and a Saber was in hot pursuit, the ban was honored almost as much in the breach as in the observance. Many MiG-15s came down on Chinese soil.

At high altitude, the Sabers were under Chinese radar surveillance for the last 100 miles (160km), which gave the Russians ample early warning. They could take off almost at leisure, climb to fighting altitude over China, then pick their moment to cross into North Korea to attack. And this in a fighter with a high-altitude performance distinctly better than that of the Saber.

There was one final tactical disadvantage. If the Americans put up a large fighter formation, the Russians could not only respond in strength if they chose, but wait until the Sabers were about to break off through lack of fuel before launching their attack. The American answer was to put up a series of four-ship flights staggered at five minute intervals. While this meant that they were often outnumbered at the beginning of an engagement, there were always supporting flights in the general area, at least some of which had ample fuel for a fight.

The dice were loaded against the Americans. Forced to operate near their ceiling, frequently outnumbered by a foe who had the assistance of radar and ground control, against a fighter which could pick its moment to attack from above then disengage in a climb that the Sabers were unable to follow, they still succeeded.

Part of the answer lay in their airplane. While the armament of the Saber was demonstrably on the light side, it was a far more stable gun platform than its opponent, especially at very high speeds, where the MiG-15 tended to snake. Its flight control system was much better, and its rate of roll was faster at all speeds and altitudes, enabling the Saber to change direction faster, and its general handling was vice-free, enabling it to be flown to its absolute limit. In a dive it could exceed Mach 1 with little difficulty.

By contrast, the MiG-15 was unstable, and suffered from severe buffeting at high Mach numbers. To guard against loss of control, the speed brakes automatically deployed at Mach 0.92. Handling left much to be desired; it was spin-prone, and tended to snap-roll out of

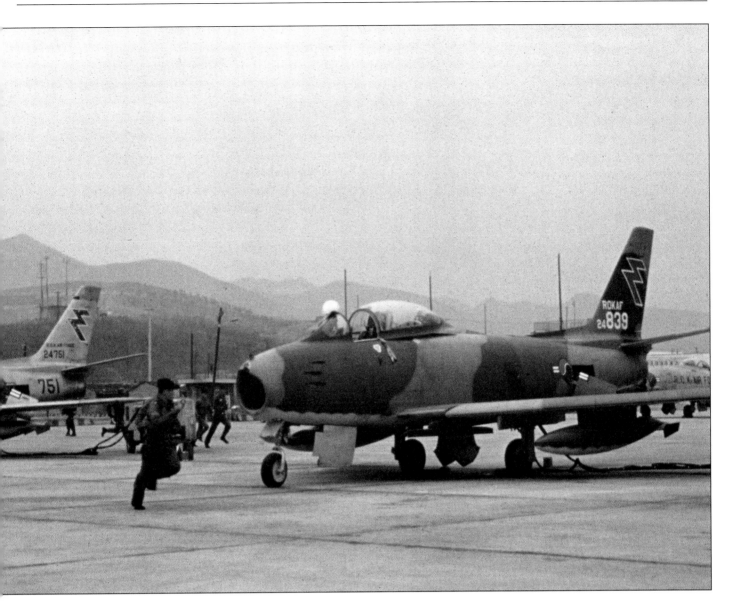

high-speed stalls. Inexperienced pilots were understandably nervous, and were unable to fly it to its limits.

THE LESSONS OF COMBAT

The Korean War conclusively demonstrated the importance of performance. The straight-winged fighters of the conflict, the F-80 Shooting Star, the F-84 Thunderjet, the F9F Panther, were all outclassed, even though the latter was powered by the advanced Rolls-Royce

Tay engine. The last two were redesigned with swept wings and tails to become the better-performing F-84F Thunderstreak and the F9F-6 Cougar respectively.

The only twin-engined day jet fighter in Korea was the Gloster Meteor F.8, flown by 77 Squadron RAAF. Although with a similar thrust/weight ratio to the MiG-15, its dated and draggy airframe badly degraded performance at altitude. After a few encounters with MiGs it was relegated to close air support.

Unusually, the nearest F-86 has been camouflaged, which seems to indicate that it has been used in the attack role. Natural aluminum was the usual finish in Korea.

EARLY SUBSONIC JET FIGHTERS

Type	Nation	Year	Speed (mph-km/hr)	Climb	Armament
Mikoyan & Gurevitch MiG-17	USSR	1950	692/1,114	5min 6sec to 32,810ft/ 10,000m	1x37mm N-37D; 2x23mm NR-23 cannon
Douglas F4D Skyray	USA	1951	695/1,118	18,000ft/min (91.44m/sec)	4x20mm Mk 12; 76 FFARs or 2 Sidewinders
Hawker Hunter	GB	1951	715/1,151	7min30sec to 45,000ft/ 13,715m	4x30mm Aden cannon
Grumman F9F Cougar	USA	1951	690/1,110	5,600ft/min (28.45m/sec)	4x20mm cannon
Dassault Mystère IVA	France	1951	696/1,120	8,860ft/min (45m/sec)	2x30mm DEFA cannon
Gloster Javelin	GB	1951	620/998	5.6min to 40,000ft/ 12,191m	2x30mm Aden cannon plus 4 Firestreak AAMs.

The Gloster Meteor F.8 was flown by 77 Squadron of the Royal Australian Air Force in Korea. Even though it had a thrust/weight ratio approaching that of the MiG-15, its draggy airframe reduced performance and it was outclassed by the Russian fighter.

Meanwhile the Russians started a trend which has continued to the present day: milking every ounce of capability from a proven design. The MiG-15 was given a larger but thinner wing with a sharper compound sweep, and other aerodynamic refinements, to become the far more capable MiG-17. Later variants were given afterburning; others were fitted with radar to give an adverse weather capability.

ANTI-BOMBER WEAPONS

The USSR had early responded to the nuclear threat. By 1950, when the USSR had demonstrated that they had both nuclear weapons and fast jet bombers, the West followed suit.

During the 1950s aircraft technology advanced faster than at any other time, and it was now that the "silver bullet" (to slay the werewolf) approach first emerged. The traditional fighter attack was made from astern with guns. At near-sonic speeds and stratospheric altitudes, maneuvrability was severely limited; a 2g turn might easily be the maximum possible. Jockeying for position behind a jet bomber was not only a lengthy business, it was also time-consuming. An attack from the front quarter was much quicker, and would negate any performance advantage the bomber held. But with closing speeds of at least Mach 1.6, visual interception was problematical. A radar-aided solution was the only one possible.

This was developed as the collision-course attack, in which the fighter was guided into radar range by ground control. Once contact

was established, the pilot locked-on his radar, keeping the contact blip within a small steering circle, and armed the system. When the computer achieved a solution, it automatically fired. The collision course attack also reduced the effectiveness of return fire from the bomber.

Guns were of little use in this scenario. Greater range and much greater hitting power was needed. Initially the preferred weapon was the 2.75in (70mm) Mighty Mouse unguided rocket, a single hit from which was almost guaranteed to bring down a heavy bomber. To compensate for lack of accuracy, it was fired in salvos of several dozen, to blanket a large area of sky, giving a high probability of at least one hit.

The theory was good; in practice it was found wanting. It was extremely difficult to keep the target within the steering circle, and if the latter took even mild evasive action it became almost impossible.

The next step was to develop homing missiles, able to follow their targets. Four methods were possible: beam-riding, semi-active radar homing (SARH), heat-homing (IR), and active radar (AR). Beam riding suffered from the same problems as collision-course interception: the pilot had to hold the radar on target to within $^1/_4$ degree for about eight seconds, which was virtually impossible for the average squadron pilot. AR was beyond the state of the art in the pre-microchip era, leaving SARH and IR as the front runners. SARH involved holding a radar lock on the target during the entire time of flight of the missile,

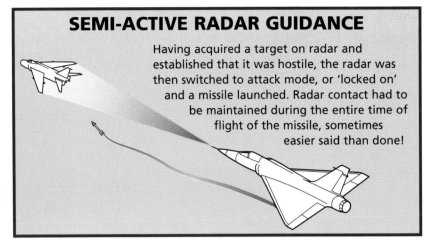

SEMI-ACTIVE RADAR GUIDANCE

Having acquired a target on radar and established that it was hostile, the radar was then switched to attack mode, or 'locked on' and a missile launched. Radar contact had to be maintained during the entire time of flight of the missile, sometimes easier said than done!

while IR produced a launch-and-leave weapon, admittedly of short range and inferior capability, but with greater intrinsic accuracy.

These finally emerged as the AIM-7 Sparrow (SARH), and the AIM-9 Sidewinder. It must be said that the British Firestreak and Red Top AAMs were both superior to Sidewinder, but the American weapon was simpler and cheaper, and consequently has continued in service to the present day, albeit in greatly improved forms.

As interception became increasingly automated, the fighter became less an airplane and more an integrated weapons system. The first fighter designed as such was the Convair F-102 Delta Dagger, which entered service in 1956, which carried six Falcons internally. Shortly after, the F-102B, later redesignated F-106 Delta Dart, entered service. With the auto-

The F-86D Saber Dog launches its full complement of unguided Mighty Mouse missiles. It is obvious that some of these weapons have started to tumble and diverge, which hardly aids accuracy. Mighty Mouse was better than nothing, but not a lot.

LOCKHEED F-104A STARFIGHTER

Dimensions: Span 21ft 11in (6.68m);
Length 54ft 9in (16.69m); Height 13ft 6in (4.11m);
Wing area 196sq.ft (18.21m²).
Power: One General Electric J79-3B afterburning
turbojet rated 14,800lb (65.78kN) static thrust maximum
power.
Weights: Empty 13,384lb (6,071kg);
Normal 22,614lb (10,258kg).
Performance: Maximum speed Mach 2.2;
Ceiling 64,795ft (19,729m); Climb 60,395ft/min (307m/sec);
Range 730 miles (1,175km).
Armament: Typically one 20mm M61 Vulcan cannon and
two AIM-9B Sidewinder heat-seeking missiles.

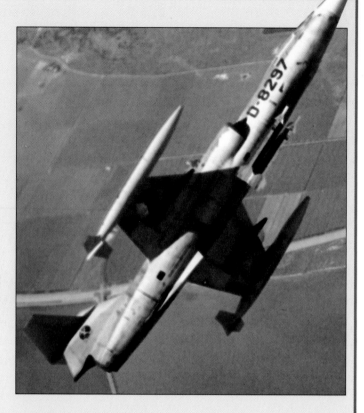

Since the very start of air combat, the advantage most
to be sought was altitude. When in Korea American F-
86 pilots found that the Russian-built MiG-15 had a
significantly better high-altitude performance, they
clamored for a fighter that could out-fly it. The result,
first flown in February 1954, was the Lockheed F-104
Starfighter. The design was optimised for high
performance; the smallest possible airframe wrapped
around the largest possible engine. An extremely sleek
fuselage with tiny thin wings and a high-set T-tail, it
was promptly dubbed -the missile with a man in it!
While handling was very precise, it was totally
unforgiving of pilot error. High wing loading

(115lb/sq.ft-563kg/m²) meant that turn capability was
poor, and it finally made its mark as a low-level bomb

The F-100 Super Saber was the first supersonic fighter to enter service anywhere in the world. Capable of Mach 1.35, it was a "hot ship", but its greatest failing was its all-gun armament.

pilot and fire control system linked to a semi-automatic ground environment (SAGE) system, which could control the interception directly from the ground, "Six" pilots thus became systems managers.

While the F-106 represented the cutting edge of technology, other developments were under way, mainly linked to aerodynamic and engine improvements. The US Navy introduced the Chance-Vought Cutlass, a strange tail-less fighter, which proved too much of a hot ship for carrier operations. Another odd Navy bird was

the Douglas F4D Skyray, a tail-less delta interceptor which could sustain climb at an angle of 70 degrees. This was designed to reach 40,000ft (12,191m) in less than five minutes. Armed with pods of Mighty Mouse rockets, it was known as the "ten minute killer", although whether this referred to the time it took to complete its mission, or the time it took to kill an inexperienced pilot, is unclear. The first supersonic Navy fighter was the Grumman F11F Tiger, a first-class if conventional jet airplane.

The first supersonic fighter to enter service, in November 1953, was the North American F-100 Super Saber. Single-engined, and with a 45 degree wing sweep and capable of Mach 1.26, it was armed with four 20mm M-39 revolver cannon. It was followed in March 1955 by the Russian MiG-19, powered by two Mikulin AM-5F axial-flow afterburning turbojets, with a wing sweep 0f 55 degrees, and capable of Mach 1.35, it was armed with three 23mm cannon, two of which were mounted in the wing roots.

Unhappy at the ability of the MiG-15 to attack from above, American pilots in Korea clamored for greater climb rates and higher ceilings. This resulted in the Lockheed F-104 Starfighter, in which the smallest possible airframe was wrapped around the biggest possible engine to give the best possible performance.

First flown in March 1954, the Starfighter was heralded as "the missile with a man in it!" It was certainly futuristic. The engine was the new General Electric J79 packaged in a beautifully streamlined fuselage with a high T-tail. Rather

EARLY SUPERSONIC JET FIGHTERS

Type	Nation	Year	Speed (Mach)	Climb	Armament
North American F-100A Super Saber	USA	1953	1.30	16,500ft/min (83.83m/sec)	4x20mm cannon
Convair F-102 Delta Dagger	USA	1953	1.25	13,000ft/min (66m/sec)	6x Falcon AAMs
Mikoyan MiG-19	USSR	1954	1.35	3min 42sec to 49,215ft (15,000m)	3x23mm NR-23 cannon
Grumman F11F Tiger	USA	1954	1.34	16,300ft/min (82.80m/sec)	4x20mm cannon
Vought F-8 Crusader	USA	1955	1.71	6min 30sec to 57,000ft (17,373m)	4x20mm cannon, 4 Sidewinder AAMs.
Saab Draken	Sweden	1955	1.80	31,000ft/min (157.5m/sec)	2x30mm Aden cannon and 4 Falcon AAMs
Dassault Mirage IIIA	France	1956	2.00	6min to 60,000ft (18,287m)	2x30mm DEFA cannon; 1x Matra 511 AAM

than swept wings, Lockheed chose running boards, very thin straight wings giving a span of just 21ft 11in (6.68m). Wing loading was very high at nearly 110lb/sq.ft (537kg/m^2), which inevitably restricted maneuverability, but this was offset by a fantastic rate of climb, sparkling acceleration, and a maximum speed of Mach 2.2. Armament was typically two AIM-9B Sidewinders and an M61A 20mm Vulcan cannon with a firing rate of 6,000 rounds per minute.

Meanwhile, what of the Europeans?

The British had introduced the subsonic Hawker Hunter day fighter, armed with four 30mm Aden cannon, and the equally subsonic Gloster Javelin all-weather fighter, a tailed delta which could carry four IR missiles. These were followed by the English Electric Lightning. Developed from a high-speed research airplane, the Lightning was capable of Mach 2, had a tremendous rate of climb, but was basically a

The first Russian supersonic fighter was the twin-engined MiG-19. Highly maneuverable, this was at first gun-armed. This is the all-weather MiG-19PM variant, armed with K-5 beam-riding air-to-air missiles.

short-range point-defense interceptor.

In France, Dassault had produced a range of post-war jet fighters, culminating in the Mirage III. A tail-less delta, this later became famous in Israeli service in the 1960s. As a home defense interceptor, it had a rocket motor to supplement climb performance, which enabled it to reach over 59,714ft (18,200m) in six minutes.

ENGLISH ELECTRIC (BAe) LIGHTNING F.6

Dimensions: Span 34ft 10in (10.62m); Length 53ft 3in (16.23m); Height 19ft 7in (5.97m); Wing area 308sq.ft (35.31m^2).
Power: Two Rolls-Royce Avon 301 afterburning turbojets rated at 16,300lb (72.4kN) static thrust each.
Weights: Empty 25,737lb (11,674kg); Normal 39,940lb (18,117kg).
Performance: Maximum speed Mach 2.14; Ceiling 57,000ft (17,373m); Climb 50,000ft/min-254m/sec; Range 802 miles/1,290km).
Armament: Typically two 30mm Aden cannon with 130rpg and two Red Top or Firestreak heat-seeking missiles.

Developed from the high-speed experimental research P.1, the Lightning was a short-range point-defense interceptor with the accent on quick reaction and fast climb. It contained many unusual features; a sharply swept wing with a straight trailing edge on which the ailerons were mounted, and two engines, staggered one atop the other which gave a frontal area little larger than that of a single-engined aircraft. Handling was superb, even without a computer between the pilot and the flight controls, while the Airpass radar could handle automated interceptions via the autopilot. The Lightning represented the high-water mark of the traditional fighter, before it was superseded by the airborne weapons system, as typified by the McDonnell Douglas F-4 Phantom II.

Combat
Around the Globe
1958-1997

T HE 1950s saw maximum speeds more than double, climb rates nearly triple, and ceilings rise by at least a quarter. Semi-automated radar-aided interception systems coupled with missiles able to home on their targets resulted in a new breed of dedicated and extremely specialized interceptors, peaking with the American F-106 Delta Dart and the Russian MiG-25 Foxbat. But even these could do no more than attempt to achieve the 100 per cent kill rate which was needed to counter nuclear-armed bombers, with little prospect of success.

To preserve the uneasy peace, deterrence looked a better prospect. Resources were poured into bigger and better bombers, largely at the expense of developing new fighters. The North American F-108 and the Republic F-103, the

latter capable of Mach 3.7, and due to fly in 1960, were both cancelled at this stage.

Meanwhile other factors had crept into the equation. Surface-to-air missiles, popularly known as SAMs, were making enormous strides. These were believed to have a very high probability of kill and were far more affordable than manned fighters.

As SAM systems improved and proliferated, the survival prospects of the manned bomber at high altitude looked slim. Electronic countermeasures offered hope but little else; Day 1 of Armageddon was a little late to be proved wrong. The bombers then did the obvious: between 1960 and 1963 they switched from high to low level, training to deliver their attack from below the radar cover. Britain and France both felt the effects of this; both had developed mixed

---

MIKOYAN MiG-25 FOXBAT

Dimensions: Span 45ft (14.02m);
Length 64ft 9½ in (19.75m); Height 18ft 4½ in (6.60m);
Wing area 661sq.ft (61.41m²).
Power: Two Tumanski R-15BD-300 afterburning turbojets rated at 11,200lb (49.78kN) each.
Weights: Empty 48,501lb (22,000kg);
Normal 80,953lb (36,720kg).
Performance: Maximum speed Mach 2.83;
Ceiling 67,917ft (20,700m); Climb 8min 54sec to 65,620ft (20,000m); Range 777 miles (1,250km).
Armament: Typically two R-40 missiles;
four R-60 missiles.

The MiG-25, codenamed Foxbat by NATO, was developed to counter the Lockheed A-12, the forerunner of the SR-71 Blackbird, and not, as was originally thought, the Mach 3-capable B-70 Valkyrie bomber. Be that as it may, the entire design was optimized for the high altitude interception mission, with high speed and rate of climb as priorities, at the expense of maneuvrability and endurance. First flown in 1964, it stretched the

contemporary Soviet state of the art to its absolute limits. Its flight control system was tied by data link to ground control, which steered it to a collision-course interception. This left the pilot as a systems manager, responsible for takeoff and landing, throttle control and missile selection and launch. In emergencies Foxbat could be accelerated to Mach 3.2, but as this wrecked the engines, it was red-lined at Mach 2.83 for normal usage.

power interceptors with a turbojet for endurance, and a rocket motor to increase climb and high-altitude performance. The rocket-assisted Dassault Mirage III had actually entered service; the Saunders-Roe SR.53 was still in the experimental stage. The former became an orthodox jet fighter; the latter was cancelled.

Another advance at this time was the miniaturization of nuclear weapons. This gave the much-neglected tactical fighter a new lease of life as an atomic bomb truck, using low level delivery, often on a one-way ticket. This, plus the service entry of homing missiles, militated against air combat maneuvring. Once more the

old parrot cry arose: "the dogfight is dead!"

It was of course true that as fighter performance expanded, the gun became less effective. The sole advance in this field was made by General Electric with the radically new 20mm M61A Vulcan multi-barrel gatling-type cannon. This provided the phenomenal rate of fire of 6,000 rounds per minute, coupled with great reliability. Yet its effective range remained much the same as its predecessors. The greater speeds and reduced turning ability of supersonic fighters made it ever more difficult to bring to bear. A fashion for gunless fighters arose, to which even the pragmatic Russians subscribed.

A Dassault Mirage IIIE of l'Armée de l'Air. The tail-less delta was in many ways ideal for high-speed high-altitude flight, but less so for maneuver combat. Despite this, the Mirage IIIC excelled for Israel when faced with Russian-built Arab fighters.

FIGHTERS IN SERVICE, 1958-1995

Type	Nation	Speed (Mach)	Ceiling (ft/m)	Climb (ft/min / m/sec)	Armament
Folland Gnat	GB	0.95	50,000/15,239	20,000/102	2x30mm Aden cannon
MiG-23MF	Russia	2.35	54,957/16,750	n/a	1x23mm GSh-23L cannon; 2xR-23R, 2xR-23T AAMs.
Dassault Mirage F.1	France	2.2	65,620/20,000	41,931/213	2x30mm DEFA cannon; 2xMatra 530F and 2xMatra R550 AAMs
Saab JA 37 Viggen	Sweden	2.0	60,042/18,300	39,963/203	1x30mm KCA cannon; 2 or 4 Sidewinders or Skyflash
Yak-38	Russia	0.95	39,044/11,900	14,961/76	2xGSh-23L cannon and 2xR-23 AAMs.
F-18C Hornet	USA	1.8	50,000/15,239	50,000/254	1x20mm M61 Vulcan cannon; 2xAIM-7 Sparrow and 2x AIM-9 Sidewinder AAMs.
Tornado F.3	GB	2.27	50,000/15,239	40,000/203	1x27mm Mauser cannon, 4xSkyflash, 4xSidewinder AAMs.
MiG-31 Foxhound	Russia	2.83	67,589/20,600	7min 54sec to 32,810ft (10,000m)	1x23mm GSh-6 cannon, 4xR-33 and 2xR-60 AAMs.
Sukhoi Su-27 Flanker	Russia	2.30	59,058/18,000	60,042/305	1x30mm GSh 30L cannon; up to 10 AAMs; AA-10 and AA-11.
Dassault Mirage 2000C	France	2.35	60,042/18,300	49,215/250	2x30mm DEFA cannon, 2xSuper 530D and 2x R.550 Magic AAMs
BAe Sea Harrier	GB	0.97	51,200/15,605	50,000/254	2x30mm Aden cannon, 4x Sidewinder or Amraam AAMs.
Dassault Rafale	France	2.0	60,042/18,300	54,924/279	1x30mm GIAT cannon, 8xMICA AAMs.

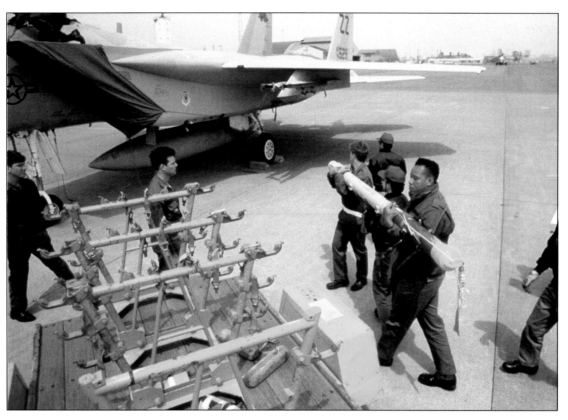

Medium range air-to-air missiles are both large and heavy. This AIM-7E Sparrow about to be loaded onto an F-15 is 12ft (3.66m) long, has a diameter of 8in (203mm), and weighs 452lb (205kg). Range is about 28 miles (44km), and all-burnt speed Mach 4.

This AAM-armed Saab J35 Draken was the most futuristic looking fighter of the 1950s. It was designed by laying out the most essential components — engine, cockpit, and avionics — and sketching in a small aerodynamic shape around them. This double-delta planform was unique.

AIR-TO-AIR MISSILES

A missile able to follow its target sounds a formidable weapon, but the reality is rather less so. Performance varies with conditions, particularly air density. On launch AAMs are boosted to maximum speed within a matter of seconds; after this they are just coasting, getting slower and slower. And as they slow, they become less maneuvrable.

AAMs reach their maximum speed and range at altitude. At sea level, speed may often reduce by half and range by one third of the maximum. The latter is also modified by intercept geometry; if the target is retreating fast, the missile may not catch it before running out of energy.

One final general point. On all early missiles the "look angle" of the seeker was limited, making a hard-maneuvring target impossible to follow. The latest generation of AAMs have wider look angles, but even then homing capability is limited by the intercept geometry at launch.

Much depends on the type of homing used. Beam-riding was quickly dropped, leaving Infra-Red (IR), Semi-Active Radar (SARH), and Active Radar (AR).

IR, or heat homing, is intrinsically the most accurate of all. Early variants could home only on a hot jet efflux, which limited them to an attack from astern. More recently their sensors have been made able to pick up hot spots on the airframe, enabling attacks to be made from any aspect. They are essentially visual-range weapons, and are balked by cloud or mist. As they are unable to discriminate between friend and foe, they are difficult to use in a confused multi-bogey situation.

SARH missiles need the parent fighter to illuminate the target with its radar; they then

AAM LAUNCH RANGE THEORY

In both cases the AAM flies 20nm (37km). From head-on, the closing speed allows it to be launched at 25nm (46km), whereas in a tail-chase a much reduced closure rate reduces this to 15nm (28km).

25 nautical mile launch range

Missile impacts

Target at launch point

Target at launch point

Missile impacts

15 nautical mile launch range

AR missiles can be used direct from close range. At medium or long range they use inertial guidance for mid-course flight, which can be updated by the parent fighter. At a pre-determined moment they switch to active radar for the terminal homing phase. AAMs are not yet infallible; they can be decoyed, jammed, and in some instances outmaneuvered, or at longer ranges, outrun. But having said that, the fighter pilot under attack has to take some form of counter-action; after all, missiles have the right of way!

FIRST USE OF AAMS

AAMs were first used in 1958, when communist PRC forces clashed with Taiwan-based Chinese Nationalists over the offshore islands of Quemoy and Matsu. On September 14, 14 Nationalist F-86F Sabers armed with Sidewinders encountered about 20 MiG-15s of the PRC. They claimed ten shot down, four with Sidewinders, although at least one claim arose when a missile was seen to closely follow a MiG into cloud. Total claims for this war, which lasted about six weeks, were 31 MiGs for the loss of just two Sabers (some sources state two F-84G Thunderjets).

home on the reflected echo. This forces the launching fighter to close the target during the entire missile time of flight, which has the effect of making it predictable. Less accurate than heat homers, they can be used from far beyond visual range, from any angle, and in most weather conditions.

The advent of the heat-seeking AAM caused two major changes in fighter tactics. Whereas a gun attack could often be defeated by diving away out of range, the greater reach of the Sidewinder made this unprofitable. Far from spelling the death-knell of the dogfight, it made turning more important than ever. Previously the basic fighter pair had flown a spacing which allowed mutual cover against gun attacks. The longer range of AAMs now made this of dubious value, and spacings increased. Over the next quarter-century, there were several limited wars which allowed fighter tactics to be refined.

INDIA VERSUS PAKISTAN

India first clashed with Pakistan in September 1965. The war was of short duration, and the ever-higher, ever-faster trend demonstrated over MiG Alley was reversed. It could hardly have been otherwise; both air forces were numerically small in relation to the length of the frontier to be covered. Nor was radar coverage comprehensive. Consequently most air fighting arose from chance encounters over the battlefield, rather than from an outright contest for air superiority.

The fighter element of the IAF consisted of 118 British-built Hawker Hunters and 80 Folland Gnats, 80 French-built Mystère IVAs, with a

small supersonic component of 10 MiG-21Fs.

To oppose them, the PAF had about 90 F-86F Sabers and a dozen F-104A Starfighters.

The Hunter was faster than the Saber, accelerated better, and with four 30mm Aden cannon packed a much heavier punch. However, it bled off speed faster in a hard turn. On the other hand, 22 Pakistani Sabers carried Sidewinders, making the IAF fighters treat all F-86Fs with great respect.

The Gnat was an attempt to break the trend of ever larger, ever more expensive fighters. Small, and armed with two 30mm Aden cannon, its performance was very close to that of the Hunter, while it was slightly more agile. In close combat, its size was a distinct advantage, as it was more difficult to spot, but at the end of the day it was a small gun-armed fighter with little potential for upgrading.

Most air fighting took place at medium and low level, often in poor visibility due to dust and haze. The two supersonic fighters played minor roles. Starfighter pilots accounted for two Mystère IVAs by day and a Canberra bomber by night, losing one of their number to a Mystère in a turning fight.

The war clearly demonstrated one thing: it was possible for subsonic fighters to survive against the Mach 2 wonders. The Gnat did well, but not exceptionally so; the lightweight fighter concept remained unproven. In air combat, PAF losses were nine – eight Sabers and one Starfighter – against IAF losses of 21, only 11 of them first-line fighters, nine Hunters and two Gnats. In all, 33 Sidewinders were launched for nine victories, a kill rate of 27 per cent. But given the predominance of maneuver combat close to the ground, this was remarkably good.

A Lockheed F-104A Starfighter of the Pakistan Air Force. In action against India it did not perform well in the dogfight, and in the second conflict it was outfought by Indian MiG-21s.

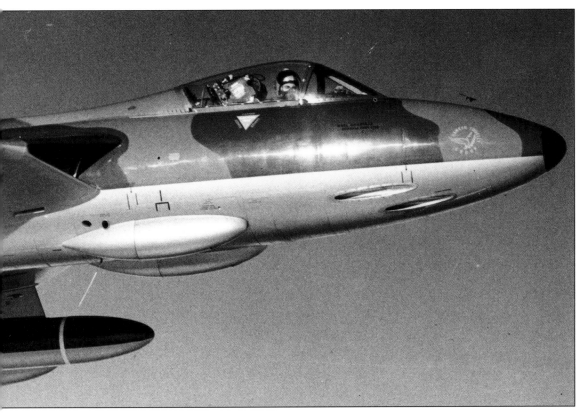

This Hawker Hunter F.6 flew with 43 and 111 Squadrons of the RAF, then was sold to India as a Mk 56A in November 1968. Able to outperform Pakistani Sabers, the balance was redressed by Sidewinder AAMs carried by the latter.

The Hunter found its true métier as a ground attack aircraft. To give quick turnaround the main armament of four 30mm Aden cannon came in the form of a pack, seen here being fitted.

The tail striping appears to indicate that this Israeli Mirage IIIC belonged to the famous 101 Squadron. The nose-high attitude on takeoff and landing is typical of tail-less deltas.

PERFORMANCE VERSUS MANEUVRABILITY

Over the next eight years, four fighter types dominated the combat arena. These were the Russian-built MiG-17 and MiG-21, the French Mirage IIIC, and the American Phantom II. Others, such as the Chinese F-6, the French Super Mystère B.2, and the American F-8 Crusader, F-100 Super Saber, F-104 Starfighter, and the F-105 Thunderchief, took lesser roles.

The MiG-17 was a transonic derivative of the MiG-15 with an afterburning engine and in some instances armed with beam-riding AA-1 AAMs. The MiG-21, which is described in detail elsewhere, was a tailed delta, very agile, with a marginal Mach 2 top speed, and often armed with two K-13A AAMs. The Mirage IIIC was a tail-less delta, agile but prone to bleed off speed alarmingly in a hard turn. Initially its missile armament consisted of a single Matra R.530 AAM. The Phantom II was a Mach 2-capable carrier fighter with bags of power but poor maneuvrability. Commonly described as "a triumph of thrust over aerodynamics", it was a twin-engined two-seater optimized for the fleet air defense role, armed with eight AAMs, but in its initial variants, no gun.

Of the secondary combatants, the F.6 was a Chinese version of the MiG-19, with twin engines and a sharply swept wing. Very agile, it was the

An RF-8A Crusader pilot ejects from his stricken jet on October 21 1961. As the gear is down, it appears that the engine has flamed out on final approach to the carrier. Ejection seats have saved the lives of literally thousands of fighter pilots over the years.

of the gunfighters", but was difficult to recover to controlled flight once it had departed. The F-100 and F-104 have been described, while the F-105, more often known as the "Thud", the heaviest single-engined single-seater fighter ever, armed with one 20mm Vulcan cannon and typically a single Sidewinder, incorporated an internal bomb bay for nuclear weapons delivery.

Between 1965 and 1973, several wars overlapped. Air combat in South-East Asia commenced in 1965 and, apart from a short hiatus at the end of the decade, lasted until January 1973. Israel clashed with its Arab neighbors in 1967, followed by the so-called War of Attrition which lasted until 1970, followed by the October War of 1973. Meanwhile India and Pakistan had once more briefly come to blows in 1971.

The most intense fighting took place between Israel and its Arab opponents. An incident on the border in April 1967 resulted in the loss of six Syrian MiG-21s. Tensions rose, and war could not long be delayed. The combined Arab air forces of Egypt, Syria, Jordan and Iraq could muster over 200 modern MiG-21s and 400 older jet fighters, plus about three dozen Tu-16 fast jet bombers. Opposing this armada were just 72 Mirage IIICJs, backed by 18 Super Mystère B.2s and 80 older types. The odds were heavy.

Then on the morning of June 6, Israel launched the now-famous pre-emptive strike.

first fighter in service to have a thrust/ weight ratio approaching unity. The SMB.2 was an orthodox subsonic swept-winged fighter, while the Crusader was a US Navy fighter, capable of Mach 1.8, and armed with 20mm cannon and up to four Sidewinders. Agile, it was known as "the last

The pre-emptive strike which started the Six Day War in June 1967 crippled the Egyptian Air Force, but did not entirely eliminate it. Here an Israeli convoy is bombed and strafed by Egyptian MiG-17s in Sinai.

Camouflage can be extremely effective in concealing aircraft, as this photograph of three F-4E Phantoms shows. The Phantom entered Israeli service during the War of Attrition, and took part in a well-planned ambush of Russian-flown MiG-21s defending Egypt.

The Egyptian Air Force was reduced to manageable proportions by the simple expedient of blowing holes in its runways, and destroying a high proportion of its airplanes on the ground. In a carefully rehearsed plan, the Israeli Air Force struck at Egypt, Syria and Jordan in quick succession, gaining a brilliant victory. The Arab nations lost an estimated 452 airplanes, 58 of them in air combat. Israeli losses were 46, ten of them in air combat. Surprisingly, all Israeli victories were claimed with the gun, even though AAMs were not only available, but used.

Meanwhile the USA had become deeply embroiled against North Vietnam. The F-105, notwithstanding its nuclear strike role, became a strategic bomber, using "iron" bombs. Initially

McDONNELL DOUGLAS F-4 PHANTOM

Dimensions: Span 38ft 5in (11.71m); Length 63ft (19.20m); Height 16ft 3in (4.95m); Wing area 530sq.ft (49.25m^2).
Power: Two General Electric J79-17 afterburning turbojets each rated at 11,870lb (5,384kg) static thrust military and 17,900lb (8,119kg) maximum.
Weights: Empty 29,535lb (13,400kg); Normal 45,750lb (20,750kg).
Performance: Maximum speed Mach 2.2; Ceiling 55,000ft (16,763m); Climb 28,000ft/min (142ft/sec); Range variable, due to external tanks and in-flight refueling, which give a radius of action in excess of 700miles (1,126km).
Armament: One 20mm M61A six-barrel cannon, and typically four AIM-7 Sparrow SARH AAMs and four AIM-9 Sidewinder IR AAMs.

Initially ordered as a fleet air defense fighter for the US Navy, able to kill from beyond visual range (BVR), the versatility of the Phantom was such that it became became an all-can-do workhorse for the USAF and many other air forces. It was fast, could carry an enormous load externally, and incorporated a weapons system which was better, because more flexible, than any other airplane of its era. It carried a two-man crew, with a weapons systems operator (whizzo) in the back seat to handle the radar and electronic magic. More powerful although less

agile, it outfought North Vietnamese MiG-17s, -19s and -21s, and gave sterling service with the Israeli Air Force against Egyptian and Syrian MiGs.

F-100s and F-104s were used in the escort role, but results were disappointing. The escort task passed to the Phantom, originally a carrier fighter but which had also become a multi-role fighter with the USAF.

The air war over North Vietnam differed considerably from every other conflict of that era. Sea-borne air power, with carriers roaming the Gulf of Tonkin, played a vital part. USAF assets based in South Vietnam were mainly engaged in what became known as the in-country war; attacks against the North were for the most part mounted by units based in Thailand, some 600 miles (965km) from the North Vietnamese capital of Hanoi. USAF Phantoms and Thuds were dependent on in-flight refueling to provide the necessary range.

Most air refueling was carried out over Laos, in full view of North Vietnamese radar. This made it impossible to conceal the approach of a strike force. The North Vietnamese Air Force had insufficient strength to oppose the combined might of the USAF and USN. Their policy was to use fighters in penny packets to disrupt American formations, and force the attackers to jettison their bombs short of the target.

Often they did not attempt to intercept at all; this made the American fighter escort a waste of resources which did little but provide extra targets for SAMs and anti-aircraft guns.

The North Vietnamese MiG-17s and MiG-21s were theoretically outmatched by the Phantoms, with their medium-range Sparrow AAMs. In practice this was more than compensated for by radar-aided ground control, which enabled the MiGs to emerge from low level in a favorable attack position. Initially the Phantoms were dependent on their on-board radar for detection, aided only by radio monitoring electronic warfare aircraft linked to Red Crown, the control cruiser USS *Chicago*, offshore.

The Americans further handicapped them-selves with a plethora of politically-inspired rules of engagement, so complicated that Phantom driver Bill Jenkins once commented to the writer that he needed a lawyer in the back seat rather than a weapons systems operator! For example, airfield attacks, which could have taken out the NVAF in short order, were for a long time forbidden! Then a wide strip near the Chinese border was placed off-limits, giving the MiG pilots a sanctuary when the going got rough. Unlike in Korea, violation of

USAF Phantoms intercept a Soviet Tu-20 Bear and escort it off their patch. This was a frequent activity during the Cold War.

The canopy of the MiG-21 opened forward to protect the pilot from windblast on ejection. A North Vietnamese pilot carries out a preflight check.

A lightweight sports car, the MiG-21 served with more air arms than any other Mach 2 fighter and saw action in several major wars. Fast and agile, it had only a limited adverse weather capability, which restricted its usefulness.

this area resulted in a court-martial.

Yet another rule, resulting from a couple of own goals, was a demand for visual identification of a target before missile launch. This instantly negated the beyond visual range capability of the Phantoms, forcing them to engage at close quarters, where the lightly wing-loaded MiG-17s and MiG-21s had the advantage.

A major problem was that the AAMs of the day had rather long minimum ranges. Once a MiG closed to within about 2,500ft (762m), it was safe from attack. The superlative Thud carried a gun, but the Phantom, responsible for its protection, did not. This was unacceptable, and gun pods were hurried into service in mid-1967. The much later F-4E was

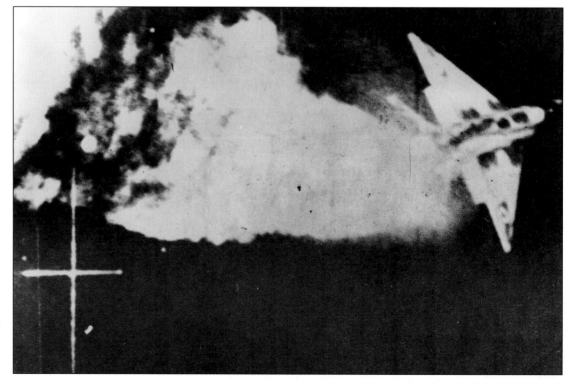

Flaps down to increase turning ability, this Egyptian MiG-21 streams flame and smoke following a gun attack by an Israeli Mirage III. Whilst the MiG-21 was in many ways the better fighter of the two, the deciding factor was pilot quality.

fitted with an internal Vulcan cannon, but this did not see action until 1972.

These factors combined to ensure that the 7½:1 kill ratio achieved over Korea was not remotely approached. Fighting was at a low level of intensity, and the kill/loss ratio was at times adverse. Operation Bolo was conceived to reverse the trend.

Bolo consisted of 56 Phantoms in two groups; West Force flew in fighter-bomber formations, using their call-signs and carrying ECM pods normally only used by F-105s. Its job was to draw up and ambush the MiGs. East Force was to cut them off from their bases and from the Chinese border.

The weather was appalling, the MiGs were slow to react, and only a dozen Phantoms of West Force made contact, shooting down seven MiG-21s with AAMs. Solid cloud foiled the best efforts of East Force.

While Bolo was an American victory, its effects were not lasting. In the seven months from August 1967, MiG-21s shot down 18 USAF fighters, losing only five of their own. Then in March 1968, American incursions over North Vietnam ceased.

Meanwhile border incidents in the Middle East commenced shortly after the end of the Six Day War, and by mid-1969 had escalated into the War of Attrition. In July 1970, events took a new and serious turn when Russian pilots in MiG-21MFs, tasked with defending Egypt, attacked Israeli Skyhawks.

The result was Operation Branch. Four Mirages penetrated the Russian-defended area south of the Gulf of Suez, and 20 MiGs were scrambled to intercept. It was an ambush; flying

low, beneath the radar cover, were four more Mirages and four Phantoms. All the Israeli pilots were experienced, with 59 victories between them. A confused maneuver fight developed, in which collision was a constant danger. Five MiGs were downed, four by missiles. The Israelis were jubilant; the Russians had been regarded as the "First Team", but had proved no better than the Egyptians! But outright conflict against Russians was internationally dangerous; a ceasefire came into effect on August 8.

Cannon shells tear up an Egyptian MiG-21 caught by a 90 degree deflection shot. This camera gun picture is usually credited to a Phantom pilot, but the head-up display is that of a Mirage IIICJ.

MIKOYAN MiG-21PF

Dimensions: Span 23ft 5½in (7.15m);
Length 44ft 2in (13.46m); Height 13ft 5½in (4.10m);
Wing area 248sq.ft (23m²).
Power: One afterburning Tumansky R11-F23-300 turbojet rated at 8,708lb (3,950kg) static thrust military and 13,492lb (6,120kg) maximum .
Weights: Empty c12,015lb (5,450kg);
Normal 17,086 (7,750kg).
Performance: Maximum speed Mach 2.05;
Ceiling 62,339ft (19,000m); Climb 40,356ft/min (205m/sec);
Range 895 miles (1,440km).
Armament: Two K-13 heat-seeking AAMs.
Later models carried the fast-firing twin-barrel 23mm GSh-23 cannon and two K-5M SARH AAMs, or two K-13s and two KM-5Ms.

First flown in February 1955, the MiG-21 was a lightweight sports car of an airplane. It was small; the author, who is not particularly tall but who could politely be described as wide, fits the cockpit like a cork in a bottle! Initially armed with two 23mm cannon, it was designed as a fast-climbing point defense interceptor, with maneuvrability which allowed it to double as an air combat fighter. Of tailed delta configuration, it was built

in 28 main variants over a period of 28 years in greater numbers than any other jet fighter, and has served with no less than 49 different air forces. Although extremely agile, it has been on the losing side in many wars. This notwithstanding, in expert hands it has proved a worthy opponent to many Western machines.

Variable-sweep wings were first adopted by Russia on the MiG-23, to combine good short-field performance with acceleration and high speed. The result was a fighter with fantastic acceleration but which turned like a tram.

In December 1971, a two-week war took place between India and Pakistan. The fighting followed the same pattern as before: skirmishes between small numbers at low and medium altitudes. Both sides admitted losses of 54, in each case this was about half the number of claims made. At last Starfighters met MiG-21s in the air. The latter, clearly capable of out-turning the Lockheed fighters, also demonstrated remarkable acceleration in shooting down four F-104As at low level, mainly with AAMs.

DISSIMILAR AIR COMBAT

Whereas performance was essential for defensive interception operations, almost all air combat in the 15 years from 1958 was essentially tactical in nature. The enormous maximum speeds were never used; supersonic time by US fighters over Vietnam totaled just a few hours; time at speeds in excess of Mach 1.6 could be measured in seconds. The fact was that the Mach 2 wonders spent most of their time at economical cruise speeds of 400-500mph (644-805km/hr). And at these speeds, they were vulnerable to the surprise bounce, and could be handily out-turned, by the lightly wing-loaded Russian sports cars.

The US Navy tackled the problem first with its dissimilar air combat training program, popularly known as Top Gun. Their solution was to use the strong points of their major fighter, the Phantom, and avoid its weak points. While Sparrow AAMs could not be used beyond visual range, on a clear day NVAF MiGs could be identified at up to eight miles (13km), which was well within the capabilities of the Phantom radar and the Sparrow. Once close combat was joined, the back-seater became an extra pair of

GRUMMAN F-14A TOMCAT

Dimensions: Span - variable sweep; 64ft 1½in (19.55m) maximum; Length 62ft 10½in (19.17m); Height 16ft (4.88m); Wing area 565sq.ft (52.50m²).
Power: Two Pratt & Whitney TF30-414 afterburning turbofans each rated at 12,350lb (5,602kg) static thrust military and 20,900lb (9,480kg) maximum.
Weights: Empty 39,921lb (18,110kg); Normal 58,571lb (26,570kg).
Performance: Maximum speed Mach 2.31; Ceiling 56,000ft (17,068m); Climb 30,000ft/min (152m/sec); Range 2,004miles (3,224km).
Armament: One 20mm M61A Vulcan cannon with 675 rounds, and either six AIM-54 Phoenix missiles or a mix of eight AIM-7 Sparrows and AIM-9 Sidewinders.

First flown in December 1970, the Tomcat was designed to replace the Phantom in the fleet air defense role. The threat had become jet bombers with long-range stand-off missiles, and to counter it the Tomcat was given an unprecedented long-range multiple kill capability. Its radar can detect targets at over 230 miles (370km) and it can track up to 24 targets and guide missiles at six of them simultaneously. On test Phoenix missiles have destroyed supersonic drone targets at launch ranges of

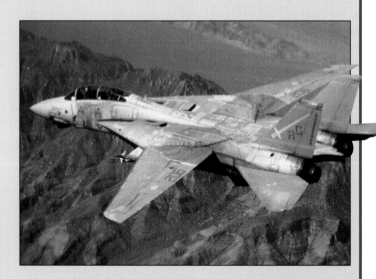

up to 127 miles (204km). A two-seater, Tomcat had to be big to carry the huge AWG-9 radar and six AIM-54s. A variable-geometry wing was adopted for maximum performance at full sweep, with a reasonably slow approach for a carrier landing. In recent years the F-14D has been given the more powerful General Electric F110 engine, and the advanced digital APG-71 radar.

eyes clearing the six o'clock area, allowing the pilot to concentrate on attack. Finally, the enormous specific excess thrust of the big fighter could be converted into acceleration, into rate of climb, and into sustaining hard turns without bleeding off speed. The secret was to keep speed in the high subsonic region where surprise was most easily attained and where turning ability was best, and not be suckered into a low-speed turning fight where the MiGs had the advantage.

The advantages of the Top Gun program were demonstrated when US air power returned to North Vietnam in 1972. Navy Phantoms improved their victory/loss ratio from 2.75:1 to 8.33:1, whereas the USAF saw only a slight improvement, from 2.15:1 to 2.83:1.

Having said that, air combat was generally of low intensity; in 5½ years of air combat, American fighter pilots claimed just 200 air combat victories for losses of 71 plus seven probables.

The final conflict of this period was again in the Middle East: the October War of 1973. Political considerations prevented a repeat of the 1967 pre-emptive strike, and the Israelis were forced to fight on the defensive. A combination of superior aircraft (Phantoms, Mirages and Neshers) and superior tactics and ability saw them gradually gain the upper hand.

With wings fully swept, the F-14A Tomcat resembles a tail-less delta. Unlike the MiG-23 it is fully maneuvrable with wings at minimum sweep. Basically a fleet air defense interceptor, the Tomcat is also a formidable opponent in close combat.

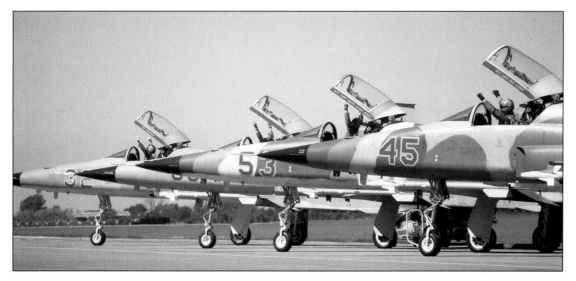

USAF dissimilar air combat training was provided by Aggressor squadrons, flying the Northrop F-5E Tiger II. This fighter was chosen for characteristics similar to the MiG-21. Seen here is the 527th Aggressor Squadron flight line at Alconbury, England.

Aware of airfield vulnerability, Sweden concentrated on off-site basing, operating from short stretches of road. The canard-delta J.37 Viggen was optimized for this task, with short take-off and landing a priority.

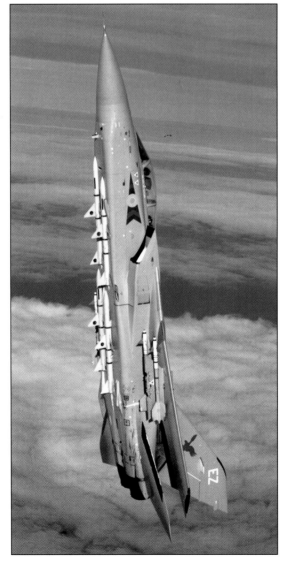

Britain needed an interceptor to combine high speed with long endurance, able to operate autonomously far out over the sea in the teeth of electronic jamming. The result was the Panavia Tornado F.3.

In 18 days of fighting, Israeli fighters claimed 335 victories, 275 of them with AAMs, mainly the Shafrir heat homer. Total admitted Israeli losses were 115, of which about 20 are believed to have fallen in air combat.

The Top Gun program, which used Northrop F-5Es and Skyhawks to simulate MiG-21s and MiG-17s respectively, had been proven. The USAF followed suit with four Aggressor squadrons; two at Nellis, one in the Philippines, and one at Alconbury in England. Not only Russian fighters were simulated, but their tactics also. Aggressor training was aimed at improving experience levels, and to this end Aggressor pilots were expected to start losing towards the end of each course. As this did not equate with fighter pilot egos, the watchword was "Be Humble". Bruce McClennan, first Aggressor commander at Alconbury, didn't quite see it that way. He amended it to "We'll Seem Humble!"

NEW IDEAS, NEW SHAPES

Wing design was inevitable a compromise, and in most early supersonic fighters the shape was optimized for high performance, at the expense of low-speed handling. The idea of a wing which could change shape to suit conditions was far from new, but until the 1960s technical problems prevented its development. Then, over about 15 years, several airplanes with variable wing sweep entered service. Some were dedicated attack and interdictor aircraft, but others were fighters beyond all doubt.

The first such fighter was the MiG-23, which entered service in 1970. It had three sweep angles: minimum for takeoff, landing and low

long range interception, but with excellent close combat capabilities. Variable-sweep wings were basically adopted to give good deck-landing qualities, but unlike the MiG-23, the Tomcat was fully stressed for maneuver at minimum sweep, making it a formidable opponent at low speeds. In two separate engagements with Libyan fighters, it has accounted for two MiG-23s and two Su-22s.

The third was the British Tornado F.3. Developed from the long-range interdiction variant, variable-sweep wings provided good short-field performance combined with long loiter time on station, coupled with high performance. A dedicated interceptor, it was designed to operate autonomously far out over the North Sea in the face of hostile countermeasures.

The most capable modern fighter is the McDonnell Douglas F-15 Eagle. An uncompromised air superiority fighter, able to deploy anywhere in the world with the help of air refueling, it performed superbly with the Israelis, and in the Gulf War.

speed flight; intermediate for cruising; and maximum for performance. Single-engined, and with a capable radar in the nose, it was unmaneuvrable, but had excellent acceleration, a maximum speed of Mach 2.35, and carried a mix of SARH and IR homing missiles.

The second was the Grumman F-14 Tomcat, a two seater fleet air defense fighter, optimized for

McDONNELL DOUGLAS F-15C EAGLE

Dimensions: Span 42ft 9¾in (13.05m); Length 63ft 9in (19.43m); Height 18ft 5½in (5.63m); Wing area 608sq.ft (56.50m²).
Power: Two Pratt & Whitney F100-220 afterburning turbofans each rated at 14,370lb (6,518kg) static thrust military and 23,450lb (10,637kg) maximum.
Weights: Empty 29,180lb (13,236kg); Normal 44,500lb (20,185kg).
Performance: Maximum speed Mach 2.5 plus; Ceiling 65,000ft (19,811m); Climb 50,000ft/min (254m/sec); Range variable with drop tanks and flight refueling.
Armament: One 20mm M61A Vulcan cannon with 675 rounds; typically four AIM-7 Sparrows (replaced by AIM-120 Amraam in 1990s), and four AIM-9 Sidewinders.

When in the late 1960s the MiG-25 Foxbat first came to the attention of the West, a comedy of errors ensued. Intelligence misinterpreted available data to conclude that it was a fully maneuvrable tactical fighter and capable of Mach 3. The Eagle, which first flew in July 1972, was designed to match it, with the slogan -not a pound for air to ground!- The result was a superlative air combat fighter, which far outclassed anything in the Russian stable in either performance or maneuvrability. A

particular innovation was HOTAS (hands on throttle and stick), in which everything needed at critical flight times, including radar mode and missile switches, were mounted on the two main controls. In air combat, the Eagle has performed superbly with the Israeli Air Force, and with the USAF in the Gulf War.

LOCKHEED MARTIN (formerly GENERAL DYNAMICS) F-16C

Dimensions: Span 31ft (9.45m);
Length 49ft 3in (15.01m); Height 16ft 7in (5.05m);
Wing area 300sq.ft (27.88m^2).
Power: One Pratt & Whitney F100-100 afterburning
turbofan rated at 14,370lb (6,518kg) static thrust military
and 23,450lb (10,637kg) maximum.
Weights: Empty 17,960lb (8,147kg);
Normal 26,536lb (12,037kg).
Performance: Maximum speed Mach 1.8;
Ceiling 50,000ft (15,239m); Climb 50,000ft/min (254m/sec);
Radius of Action 576 miles (926km).
Armament: One 20mm M61A Vulcan cannon; typically two
or four AIM-9 Sidewinders, AIM-120 Amraam, or Pythons.

The enormous costs of the huge and tremendously capable Tomcat and Eagle made them unaffordable in sufficient numbers. The USAF solution was the hi-lo mix, small and affordable airplanes to back up the expensive superfighters. The result was the F-16, which was first flown in January 1974. Properly called the Fighting Falcon, but universally known to those who fly it as the Viper, the F-16 was given superb maneuvrability to suit the close combat mission. Computerized fly-by-wire gave carefree handling; the view from the cockpit was outstanding, while the Viper could sustain a 9g turn over a small portion of the envelope. To aid pilot resistance to high-g, the heel line was set high, and the seat raked back to a steep angle. Another innovation was a side-stick controller. Sold to many countries around the world, the Viper has also proved itself in the attack role.

The dual-role fighter/ attack F/A-18 Hornet. Its cockpit, the first to use display screens instead of dials, was at the time the ultimate in man/machine symbiosis.

More orthodox fighters also entered service at about this time. The best of these was the McDonnell Douglas F-15 Eagle, described elsewhere, which led the field for many years. But like the Tomcat, the Eagle was unaffordable in the numbers required, and a new lightweight fighter was needed to back it.

Two new airplanes competed, and the winner was the General Dynamics F-16. This combined a host of new features, notably relaxed stability and fly-by-wire, which gave it unparalleled agility. It also happened that the loser, the Northrop F-17, was adopted by the US Navy as a multi-role fighter to supplement the Tomcat

and replace the Phantom and Corsair in the attack role. Not only was it more carrier-compatible than the F-16, but it offered greater development potential and, for operations far out over the ocean, twin-engined safety.

Navalized by McDonnell Douglas to become the F-18 Hornet, it was the first of the "glass-cockpit" fighters, in which the old-fashioned "steam-gauge" instruments were replaced by screens on which all relevant information could be called up at the touch of a button. As such, it set the trend for all future fighters.

At supersonic speeds the centre of lift moves aft. On a tail-less delta machine this adversely affects maneuvrability, while during hard turns the induced drag rise bleeds off speed at an alarming rate. Aware of these shortcomings on the Mirage III, Dassault produced the Mirage F.1, an orthodox swept-wing fighter. Performance and maneuvrability were improved, but not by a tremendous amount.

With the advent of relaxed stability and computerized fly-by-wire, Dassault returned to the tail-less delta planform with the Mirage 2000, combined with a variable-camber wing. This cured the worst problems of the delta planform, giving lift where formerly there was drag, and producing a superb high-altitude fighter which entered service in 1984.

MORE WARS

The combat debut of the F-15 came on June 27 1979, when a mixed force of Israeli Eagles and Kfirs encountered between eight and 12 Syrian MiG-21s over Lebanon. F-15s accounted for four MiGs and a Kfir one. Other clashes followed, then on March 13 1981 a Syrian MiG-25 was shot down by an Eagle, the first time one of these super-fast interceptors had been defeated.

Matters came to a head in June 1982 over the Beka'a. Having first knocked out the Syrian radar and missile systems, Israeli F-15s and

F-16s, controlled by E-2C Hawkeye AEW airplanes, using radar "shadows" in which to conceal their presence until the moment of attack, scored a resounding 84-0 victory, mainly over MiG-21s and MiG-23s.

On the far side of the world, in the storms and fog of the South Atlantic, British and Argentine fighters were in action. The British fighter was the Sea Harrier, a subsonic vectored thrust carrier fighter, armed with a 30mm Aden cannon and two AIM-9L Sidewinders. They were pitted against supersonic Mirage IIIs armed with 30mm DEFA cannon and two R.550 Magic IR AAMs. Other Argentine airplanes were Daggers, which were homebrew Israeli Mirages, plus Skyhawk light attack bombers.

The IAI Kfir C.7 was a reverse-engineered Mirage IIIC, modified to accept the GE J79 engine, with improvements such as canard foreplanes. This was an emergency measure intended to reduce reliance on French or US sources for warplanes.

BAe Sea Harriers of the Royal Navy, and Harrier GR.3s of the RAF, seen at Ascension Island en route to the South Atlantic in 1982. This was the war in which the concept of short takeoff and vertical landing aircraft proved itself.

Aware of the shortcomings of the tail-less delta configuration, the next Mirage was the more conventional F.1, seen nearest the camera. In the background is the Anglo-French Jaguar attack aircraft.

Much has been made of the ability of Sea Harriers to perform unorthodox maneuvers by vectoring their thrust; in this conflict it was not used. The bombing of the runway at Port Stanley by a Vulcan caused the only dedicated Argentine air combat unit to be withdrawn to protect the mainland, and from that time air combat was restricted to the interception of fighter-bombers, mainly at low level. As the British had no airborne early warning aircraft, this was not as effective as it might have been, and the ships of the Royal Navy paid a heavy price. The final air combat score was 23 to nil in favour of the Sea Harriers.

In the Gulf War of 1991, Iraq took on the might of the Western powers. It was a foolish trick; Iraq's only really modern fighter was the MiG-29, which dated from 1977. The others were antiquated MiG-21s and Mirage F.1s, and the unmaneuvrable MiG-23s and MiG-25s. They were opposed by British Tornado F.3s, French Mirage 2000Cs, USAF F-15Cs and F-16Cs, and USN F-14s and F-18s, backed by EA-6 and EF-111 electronic warfare aircraft, E-2C and E-3 Sentry AWACs machines, all supported by more tankers than they could shake a stick at!

The MiG-29 was an air combat fighter designed to be able to take on the best of the Americans: the F-15, F-16 and F-18. It was tremendously agile, with a high thrust to weight ratio giving excellent performance, and carried up to six SARH and IR AAMs. A helmet-

MIKOYAN MiG-29 FULCRUM

Dimensions: Span 32ft 3½in (11.36m); Length 56ft 8¾in; Height 15ft 6¼in (4.73m); Wing area 409sq.ft (38m²).
Power: Two Klimov RD-33 afterburning turbofans each rated at 11,111lb (5,040kg) static thrust military and 18,298lb (8,300kg) maximum.
Weights: Empty 22,487lb (10,200kg); Normal 33,598lb (15,240kg).
Performance: Maximum speed Mach 2.3; Ceiling 55,777ft (17,000m); Climb 64,964ft/min (330m/sec); Range 932 miles (1,500km).
Armament: One 30mm GSh-30L cannon with 150 rounds; six AAMs including a mix of SARH and IR AA-10 and AA-11.

First flown by the late Alexandr Fedotov in October 1977, the MiG-29 was designed as an agile air combat fighter to counter the American F-16 and F-18. It contained a number of innovative features, not the least of which was a system of engine doors which could be closed on takeoff to guard against ingestion of things which might damage the compressor. These could also be closed in flight, although the value of this is problematical. Another innovation was a helmet-mounted sight, which allowed missiles to be launched at high (45 degree) off-boresight angles. While it has often been suggested that these could be used against rear-quarter targets, this does not appear to be the case. In service with the Luftwaffe, Fulcrum has proved to lack endurance and is difficult to maintain.

The mighty MiG-31 Foxhound is a two-seater developed from the MiG-25 to counter the threat of cruise missiles. Very fast but not agile, it has been flown over the North Pole by Mikoyan chief test pilot Roman Taskayev.

AIR TO AIR HOMING MISSILE PERFORMANCES

Type	Nation	Mach No	Range (miles/km)	Homing	Year
AIM-9B Sidewinder	USA	2.5	2/3.2	IR	1956
AIM-4B Falcon	USA	3.0	6/9.65	IR	1956
K-13 Atoll	Russia	2.5	4/6.4	IR	1961
Red Top	GB	3.2	71/2/12	IR	1964
R-23R Apex R-23T Apex	Russia	3.5	20/32 9.3/15	SARH IR	1973
AIM-54 Phoenix	USA	5.0	92/148	inert/AR	1973
R.550 Magic	France	2.0	6/10	IR	1975
AIM-7F Sparrow	USA	4.0	62/100	SARH	1977
AIM-9L Sidewinder	USA	2.5	11/18	IR	1977
Sky Flash	GB	4.0	31/50	SARH	1978
AA-9 Amos	Russia	4.0	31/50	inert/AR	1984
Super 530D	France	4.6	25/40	SARH	1985
Python 3	Israel	2.5	91/2/15	IR	1986
MICA	France	3.5	31/50	AR/IR	1990
AIM-120 Amraam	USA	5.0	47/75	inert/AR	1992

mounted sight gave the Archer dogfight missiles a high off-boresight capability. The 30mm GSh-30L cannon had a unique sighting system, linked to both an IR sensor and the radar, one taking over from the other automatically.

Once battle was joined, the technical superiority of the Western powers was supreme. The Iraqi radar and communications system was largely wrecked in the first few hours, and the few Iraqi aircraft to seek action flew unsupported. They were tracked from the moment they left the ground, and hunted down.

Despite their superiority, the Western fighters scored only 34 victories, most of them at night. This was mainly due to lack of opportunity, as most Iraqi fighters took care to keep well out of the way. Aggressive Iraqi pilots were rarely encountered.

MODERN RUSSIAN FIGHTERS

In addition to the MiG-29, two more Russian fighters had emerged. The MiG-31 Foxhound is a two-seater interceptor developed from the MiG-25, specifically to counter cruise missiles, and like the Tomcat has a multiple kill capability. Operational from 1982, it has a long-range radar with a phased-array antenna, and is stated by Chief Test Pilot Valeri Menitsky to be able to detect stealth aircraft, although at what range is not known. Main armament is four long-range R-33 AAMs, and a six-barrel 23mm GSh-6-23 cannon. Information is exchanged between aircraft via data link.

Looking like an overgrown MiG-29, the Sukhoi Su-27 first flew in May 1977, but underwent extensive redevelopment before reaching the operational units. The Russian equivalent of the F-15, the Su-27 is huge, very capable, and carries up to 10 AAMs. Internal fuel capacity is massive, giving very long range without having to use drag-producing external tanks. It is also, as it has demonstrated since 1989, capable of some most unusual maneuvers. Development of this massive fighter is continuing.

Even bigger than the F-15 Eagle, Sukhoi's Su-27 Flanker represents the pinnacle of Russian fighter design. Able to carry up to 10 AAMs, it can perform unorthodox maneuvers in the hands of a skilled pilot.

The Future
of Air Combat

WHILE WARFARE is generally described as the second oldest profession, fighter combat is its newest, and most complex, manifestation. The eight decades since Frantz and Quenault scored the first air victory have seen an unbroken succession of technical advances, in aerodynamics, propulsion, detection systems, and weaponry. The two young Frenchmen would have regarded the capabilities of the modern fighter as magical. In fact, the modern Americanism "the silver bullet" solution, to make every fighter pilot an ace through superior technology, is not far short of the mark.

A few fighters have become immortal: the Sopwith Camel and the Fokker D.VII in the First World War; the Spitfire, the Mustang and the FW 190A in the Second; the F-86 Saber over Korea; the Phantom in a score of conflicts around the world. All have since been supplanted. Today's best – the F-15 Eagle and the F-16 Viper; the incredible Russian Su-27 Flanker; even Rafale and the Eurofighter 2000 – will all in due course pass away, supplanted by fighters with capabilities which we can only dream about.

What of the future? At present, fighters are dependent on force multipliers: specialized jamming airplanes to defeat enemy radar and detection systems; AWACs aircraft to control the battle from a distance; and tankers to extend effective range.

Two factors have recently emerged to change the status quo. Stealth makes jamming airplanes less necessary, while new long-range AAMs may well make AWACS and tankers too vulnerable for use against a hi-tech threat.

BEYOND VISUAL RANGE COMBAT

Two forms of combat are visualized for the future: beyond visual range, and close combat, i.e. dogfighting. Of these, the former is optimized to the "silver bullet" solution, in which superior technology plays the greater part. At its most advanced, it works thus.

AWACS or ground radar detects a threat at long range and positively identifies it as hostile. This can be done in a variety of ways: tracking the enemy formation from its home base; triggering its Identification Friend/Foe (IFF) device; or by non-co-operative target recognition technology, in which the radar characteristics of the contact enable it to be identified.

The information is fed to the nearest friendly fighters via secure data link. They turn on to an interception course, with their on-board radars on stand-by; i.e. not emitting. Using radar actively will of course reveal their presence, and

Eurofighter 2000, developed for Britain, Germany, Italy and Spain, is a close-coupled canard delta with relaxed stability for great maneuvrability. It carries a mix of AAMs for both beyond visual range and close combat.

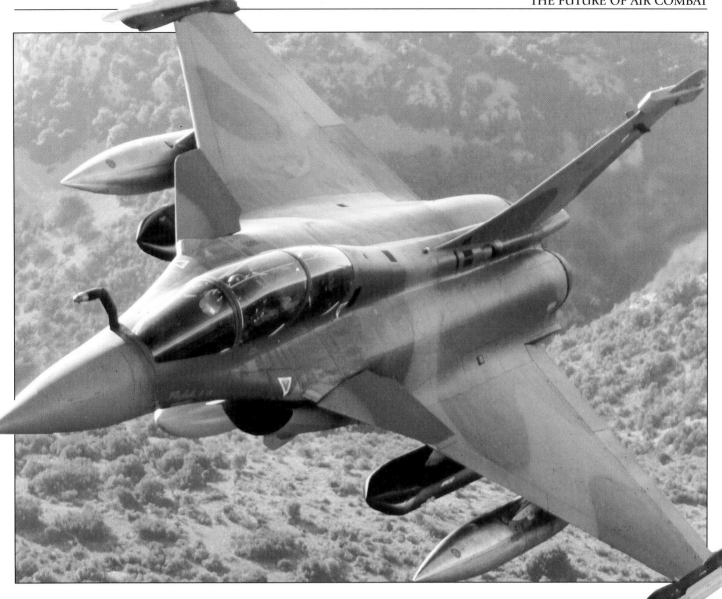

Another European close-coupled canard delta is Dassault's Rafale, for l'Armée de l'Air and the Aeronavale. Smaller and lighter than Eurofighter 2000, the main version will be a two-seater.

the element of surprise will be lost. Target data is then fed through the system from AWACS or GCI, and medium-range AAMs are readied and launched on a preset course using strap-down inertial navigation. At a given point, the radar seekers of the AAMs activate for the terminal homing phase, giving only a few seconds warning to the enemy. The surviving hostile airplanes, having lost some of their number to the AAMs, are immediately thrown on the defensive and break in all directions. At this point the attackers switch their radars into search and track mode to hunt them down, still from beyond visual range.

The theory is neat; the practice less certain. Even quite a moderate change of course by the enemy may well put them outside the look angle of the AAM's seeker when the terminal homing stage is reached. Also, against a hi-tech opponent, the air will be full of jamming.

Stealth, or the art of low-observables, is a potential factor here. In its most advanced forms, it can easily reduce radar detection range to a quarter, or even one fifth, of its original value. This will obviously degrade the value of AWACs or GCI by a significant amount. Contrary to some things that have been written, there is as yet no such thing as a radar-invisible

airplane, nor is there likely to be in the foreseeable future. A small radar signature, certainly. A small heat signature, equally certainly. But there is no way that the visual signature can be reduced to any great extent, and the stealth aircraft will therefore always be vulnerable to the fighter pilot who presses on in true Richthofen mode, to search visually.

In defensive operations many advantages lie with the defenders. They operate in a friendly environment: ground radar and GCI; friendly counter-measures; and ground defenses, guns and SAMs. But not all fighter operations are defensive. It is often necessary to carry the fight to the enemy. Over the battlefield can normally be considered neutral sky, but once beyond this

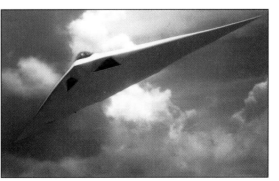

Stealth is now a very important factor in combat. This proposal for a stealthy carrier attack aircraft for the US Navy has since been abandoned.

Even attack aircraft are armed for self-defense, and cannot be taken lightly by the fighter community. Here a Tornado GR.3 of 15 Sqn RAF lets fly with an AIM-9L Sidewinder.

A French Mirage 2000-5 routinely carries four Mica radar-homing and two R550 Magic heat-homing missiles in the air defense role. Three massive drop tanks give extra endurance.

area the advantages lie with the enemy. It should not be forgotten that in the limited wars of the past the vast majority of casualties have fallen to ground fire of one sort or another. In the Gulf War of 1991, only one Coalition airplane is believed to have fallen to Iraqi fighters; an F-18 Hornet may well have been shot down by an AAM from a MiG-25.

ECM is all very well, but in recent years another method has come to the fore, which is equally effective against SAMs and AAMs. This is supercruise, the ability to sustain high supersonic speeds without afterburning, typically something in excess of Mach 1.5.

The more capable SAMs are generally dependent on radar for early detection. Having acquired a target they are launched, but take time to accelerate to operational altitude. In this case, stealth reduces detection distance, while supercruise crimps in the warning time. The combination makes it difficult, if not absolutely impossible, for the missile to track and home on a target moving at upwards of 1,450ft/sec (442m/sec), in thin air where the SAM's maneuver capability is greatly reduced.

By the same token, the problems of fighter interception are greatly increased. Getting into an attack position is extremely problematical; the extreme closing speeds in a front quarter attack pose fuzing problems for AAMs, whilst from astern the effective range is so fore-shortened by extreme speed that an interceptor stands little chance of achieving an effective firing position.

CLOSE COMBAT

There is a school of thought which maintains that close combat is the way to go. Of course, while stealth may not entirely rule out BVR combat, it will make visual range combat far more likely. What then are the basic requirements for this?

Basic fighter armament still consists of AAMs and the gun. The latter is effective to a range of perhaps 1,500ft (457m), but it is instantly available, and the only countermeasure against it is hard maneuvring. But, discounting a lucky shot, an average of several hits of 30mm, and rather more of 20mm, are required to inflict lethal damage on a modern fighter. Even though a six-barrel cannon can spew out shells at the rate of 100 per second, the target may be aligned for only a fraction of this time, and sufficient hits cannot be assured.

A future answer to this may be the Barrel-Launched Adaptive Munition (BLAM). Currently under development, these contain a miniaturized guidance system which enables them to follow a maneuvring target. A sensor in the nose uses laser homing to adjust its angle,

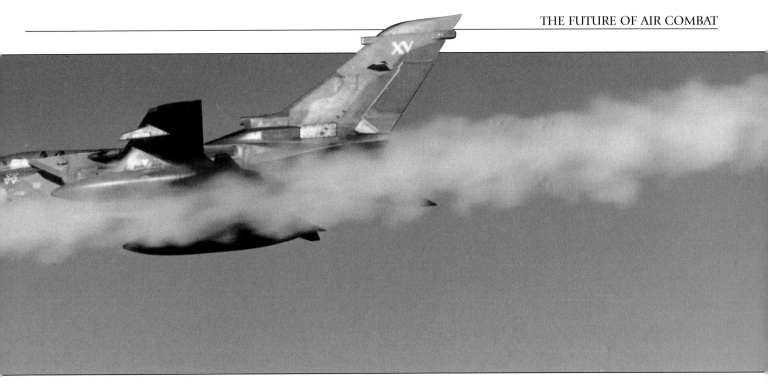

and maneuver, allowing the shell to follow its target. This is all very well, but the main difficulty is keeping the laser designator trained unerringly on a hard-maneuvring target. If it works as advertised, this should come close to doubling effective gun range, but inevitably several hits will be required to assure a kill. This is far from certain. Whether the BLAM will prove to be a viable weapon of war remains to be seen. Like so many other bright ideas, it may well be found wanting in practice.

The IR-homing missile remains the primary fighter weapon for the foreseeable future. It is small and light, and imposes little performance penalty on the parent fighter. Early IR seekers were easily fooled or decoyed, but the latest Imaging Infra-Red (IIR) heads are far more reliable. A "fire and forget" weapon, once it is on its way it needs no further assistance, and the fighter can maneuver freely. Like all modern fighter weapons (with the exception of a rearward-firing missile unveiled by the Russians in 1995), it points forward, in the direction of flight. To launch, the fighter has to go boresight (point its nose in the rough direction of the target).

In recent years, AAMs have appeared with a significant off-boresight capability, notably the Russian R-73, which has an off-boresight angle of 60 degrees. This takes it well outside the angle of the conventional head-up display used for cueing missiles, and requires a complex helmet-mounted sight to aim it.

Like all missile shots, capabilities are modified by the intercept geometry and dynamics (relative speeds and angles of fighter and target), and in practice 45 degree off-boresight seems to be about the useable limit. In peacetime exercises it seems pretty effective, and is far better than the latest Sidewinder but, in the stress of real war, things have a habit of

The Advanced Short Range Air to Air Missile (ASRAAM) will replace the Sidewinder in RAF service. Hypersonic, and with a wide offboresight look angle, ASRAAM uses imaging infra-red homing combined with software-based image processing against countermeasures.

Fighter maneuvers have traditionally been based on a combination of energy and lift. The MBB/Rockwell X-31 was designed to add thrust vectoring into the equation, which allowed previously impossible maneuvers to be carried out, such as the 'square corner' shown here.

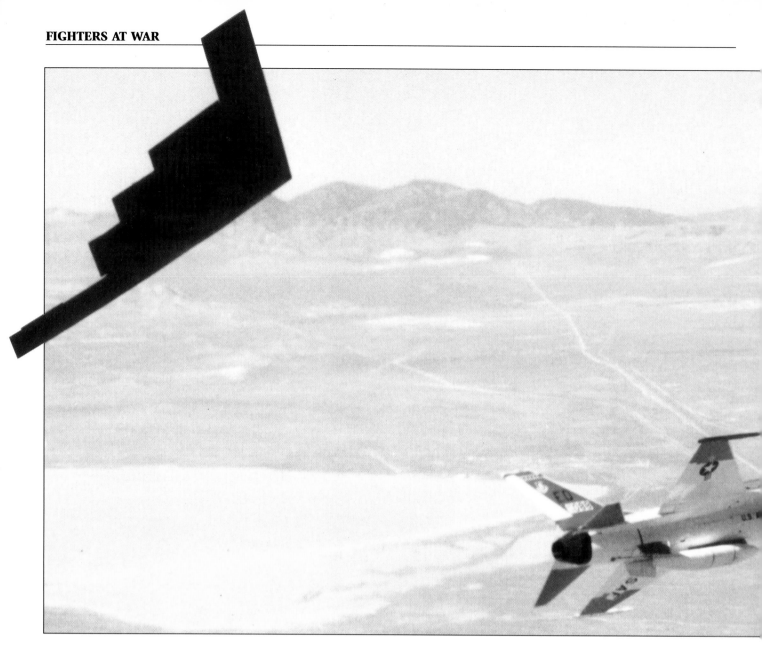

Accompanied by an F-16 chase plane, the weird shape of the B-2 stealth bomber banks over the Nevada desert. Its tiny radar signature and diffuse exhaust make it difficult to detect by conventional means, and almost impossible to intercept.

springing a leak. For example, prior to Vietnam, Sparrow and Sidewinder regularly achieved very high kill probabilities; in battle Sparrow rated about 8 per cent and Sidewinder 15 cent!

Work is currently proceeding to improve off-boresight capabilities; Hughes Missile Division demonstrated a gimbal limit of 120 degrees in the early 1980s, but this was very complicated and expensive. On the other hand, a 90 degree angle is entirely practical, and this will feature on the British Aerospace Asraam.

The helmet-mounted sight naturally allows an all-round view limited only by the pilot's neck. This has given rise to speculation that AAMs can be launched "over the shoulder" at targets in the rear hemisphere. While there would be no real difficulty in getting a missile to turn through the required angle after launch, problems arise in that the seeker would have to acquire the target in mid-flight. The very thought makes wingmen unhappy; where do they hide when the leader is spraying missiles around astern? It will probably take at least ten years to solve this rather fascinating technical and tactical problem, and even then it may well take an active radar seeker to do it rather than an undiscriminating heat homer.

Close combat has traditionally commenced with a high-speed slashing attack followed by heavy maneuvring, but the advent of agile high off-boresight missiles has called the latter into question. The maneuvring powers of very agile missiles are not constrained by the limitations of a human pilot, while high off-boresight capability largely removed the need for the pilot to hoick the nose of his fighter around to get a valid shot. Does this mean that maneuvrable fighters have become much less important?

It will be remembered that the first homing missiles, far from making maneuver combat redundant, made turning more important than ever before. This will also be the situation in the future.

When under missile attack, the pilot will not only deploy all the countermeasures at his command, he will also endeavor to evade by turning as hard as possible. While an airplane capable of a 9g turn may seem mismatched against a missile that can pull 30g, the situation is less onesided than it appears. Turn capability is largely related to speed; 30g at Mach 4 gives a quite modest turn rate and radius, easily beaten by many fighters at subsonic speeds. The priority is to create as much angle-off as possible to make

The 'Big Picture' cockpit, developed by McDonnell Douglas, shows all necessary data on a single tactical display screen. Information is called up by the pilot as required, while the presentation sizes are variable.

Modular Aircrew Simulation System is a flight training system. Here it is configured as the F/A-18 Hornet. It can also be reconfigured to simulate the F-15 Eagle, the AV-8B Harrier, or virtually any other tactical aircraft, by changing the software.

the missile work hard and hopefully fail. Conversely, even with off-boresight weapons, the fighter pilot should always seek a heart of the envelope shot, to maximize kill probability.

STEALTH

Stealth has always been with us, but only in the last few decades has it matured enough to become really useable. The first attempt dates back to 1916, a Fokker Eindecker covered with transparent sheeting. The next decades were restricted to the use of camouflage schemes intended to reduce visibility. Then, with the jet age, radar signature became increasingly important, and the SR-71 had many radar-reducing features. In recent times these have been refined into careful shaping, internal carriage of all fuel and weapons, curved inlet ducts to shield the compressor face of the engine, and the extensive use of radar-absorbent materials. Active radar emissions are kept to an absolute minimum and efforts have been made to reduce the heat signature from the engines.

Remaining undetected is a major key to successful air combat and stealth provides this in full measure. Detect first and shoot first is the watchword, and stealth, combined with the

latest communication aids from outside sources, is here to stay. Only a quantum leap in detection technology can defeat it.

SUPERMANEUVRABILITY

Over the years, technical advances have pushed the fighter performance envelope ever onwards and outwards. But while speeds, climb rates and ceilings increased, turn rates suffered. Back in 1917, German ace Werner Voss could reef his Fokker Triplane round at 45deg/sec. Some 50 years later, the MiG-21 could barely manage 14deg/sec. While matters have improved in recent years, anything over 20deg/sec is considered pretty good.

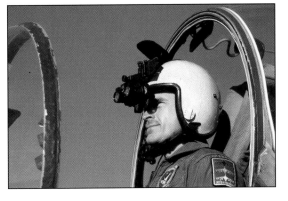

Night operations, especially at low level, often call for the pilot actually to see where he is going, rather than rely on artificial means. Night Vision Goggles, as seen here, provide this.

139

The Sukhoi Su-37 is fitted with thrust-vectoring nozzles which allow it to perform some amazing maneuvers. This is the routine flown by test pilot Eugeny Frolov at Farnborough 1996. It includes the Super Cobra and the Kulbit.

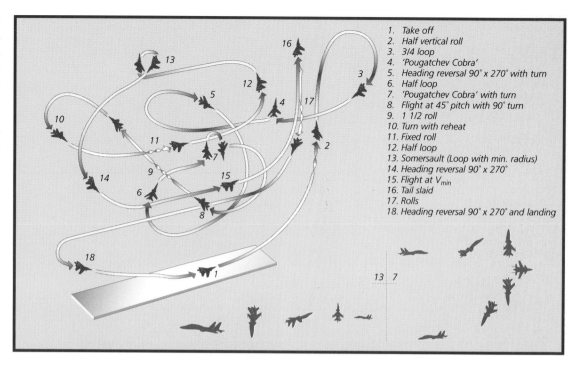

1. Take off
2. Half vertical roll
3. 3/4 loop
4. 'Pougatchev Cobra'
5. Heading reversal 90° x 270° with turn
6. Half loop
7. 'Pougatchev Cobra' with turn
8. Flight at 45° pitch with 90° turn
9. 1 1/2 roll
10. Turn with reheat
11. Fixed roll
12. Half loop
13. Somersault (Loop with min. radius)
14. Heading reversal 90° x 270°
15. Flight at V_{min}
16. Tail slaid
17. Rolls
18. Heading reversal 90° x 270° and landing

Frolov brings his huge fighter in to land after his impressive display at Farnborough in 1996. A former member of the Soviet Aerobatic Team, he maintains that the Super Cobra and the Kulbit are valid combat maneuvers, and it would be hard to refute this.

The limiting factor in maneuver flight has traditionally been lift. Minimum flying speed (V_{min}) is the speed at which just enough lift is generated to hold the airplane in the air in straight and level flight. In the thinner air at altitude, V_{min} naturally increases. A V_{min} of 150mph (241km/hr) at sea level becomes 384mph (618km/hr) at 50,000ft (15,239m).

Turning aggravates the situation. V_{min} increases by the square root of the g pulled in the turn; therefore a mere 4g turn at 50,000ft (15,239m) would double it to 768mph (1,236km/hr). The point here is that at very

The Sukhoi Su-27 Flanker has an unusual feature in its simply enormous internal fuel tankage which, in the overload condition, cuts out the need for drop tanks, leaving all hard points free for missiles. This example is from the Ukrainian Air Force.

high altitudes, maneuver capability becomes increasingly limited by lack of lift and lack of aerodynamic control. If some means could be found of providing control below V_{min} levels, this would open up a large wedge of the envelope which was previously unusable, giving a fighter so equipped a tremendous advantage over conventional opponents.

A few early advances had already been made. Control during the hover (well below V_{min}), had been achieved by bleed air puffers, while a few special Starfighters had been equipped with hydrogen peroxide thrusters to allow control at ultra-high altitudes. These systems were inadequate for combat maneuvers, but Dr. Wolfgang Herbst, a German engineer, conceived the idea of vectored thrust as a method of control at speeds below V_{min}.

The result was the MBB/Rockwell X-31, an experimental airplane capable of post-stall maneuvrability, later to be known as super-maneuvrability. Exhaustive trials showed the X-31 to be capable of totally unorthodox and previously impossible gyrations which were demonstrated at Le Bourget in 1995. In close combat these gave it a tremendous advantage over conventional fighters.

The next step was to apply this principle to existing airplanes. First was the F-16, already a byword for orthodox maneuvrability. Trials showed that thrust vectoring enhanced its capabilities out of all recognition. The helicopter turn allows the F-16 MATV to spiral down at the centre of an attacking fighter's maximum rate turn, keeping its nose on target all the way, while the MATV can generally stay out of trouble even in a two versus one scenario against F-16Cs.

Meanwhile the Russians got in on the act. At Le Bourget in 1989, Sukhoi Su-27 test pilots Viktor Pugachev and Eugeny Frolov had demonstrated ultra-high angle of attack flight with the Cobra maneuver. Although not a valid

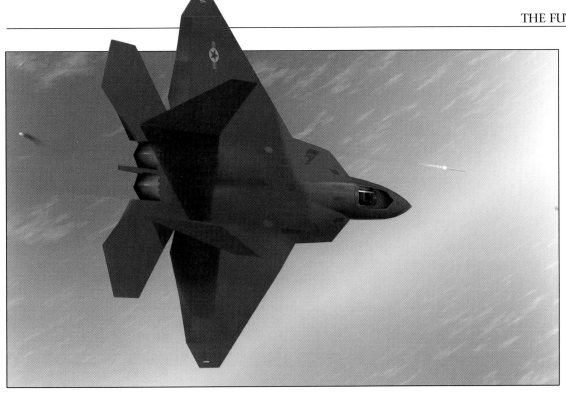

Computer-generated image of the Lockheed F-22 Raptor. The need for stealth means that all weaponry is carried in internal bays. Successor to the F-15 Eagle, it will be the world's best fighter for at least the next decade.

combat maneuver, it showed controllability well beyond the norm. The canard-equipped Su-35 followed with the Hook, basically a Cobra in the horizontal plane.

Then at Farnborough '96, Eugeny Frolov demonstrated the thrust-vectoring Su-37 with maneuvers that were almost unbelievable; the Super Cobra, in which an angle of attack of 135 degrees was reached, followed by a recovery to the vertical position which was sustained for several seconds, then a pitch-back into level flight. While this was sensational, the Kulbit that followed was incredible. The big Sukhoi was pulled through 180 degrees, to face in the opposite direction inverted. There it was stabilized for a second or two before thrust vectoring was used to complete the somersault, coming out 30 degrees nose-low with just 37mph (60km/hr) on the clock, but under perfect control.

What Frolov had convincingly demonstrated was pointability, the ability to hoick the fighter's nose around at high angles of attack before stabilizing for long enough to poop off a missile. The combination of this and agile off-boresight AAMs seems a formidable one, which will bring another dimension to close combat.

Currently the USA is developing two main fighter types: the Lockheed F-22 Raptor, which has supercruise, stealth, and thrust vectoring; and the Joint Strike Fighter, the design of which has yet to be finalized, but which represents the affordable end of an advanced hi-lo mix, and at least one version of which will be capable of vertical takeoff and landing.

SUMMARY

The past is littered with predictions about the shape of air combat, most of them wrong. While the future is unclear, it seems that stealth, combined with increasingly clever ECM, will largely negate BVR combat, making knife-range visual engagements ever more likely. A combination of agile airplanes and agile missiles will make this a very dangerous environment.

What is desperately needed to make it survivable is improved situational awareness. A total "glass cockpit" has already been demonstrated, with a touch-sensitive screen on which information can be called up at will. Pilot's Associate is something else for the future, where a computer advises the human pilot of the best course of action to take in certain situations. Of course, this will simply play the percentage solutions, with no equivalent of human strokes of unorthodox genius. Flight control computers which are able to reconfigure the system to compensate for a degree of battle damage are yet another possibility. Then of course we have the unmanned fighter, completely automated, but with a human controller far away in an underground bunker. But this last is fortunately very far off.

Lockheed Martin's proposal for the Joint Strike Fighter. Stealth and vectored thrust will be incorporated. One variant will be capable of vertical take-off and landing, using a system totally different to that of the Harrier.

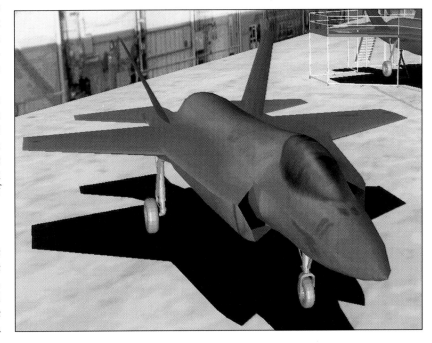

Index

Picture Credits

Jacket and front matter: Front, Francois Robineau (Dassault/Aviaplans), via Aviation Photographs International (API); back (main pic), McDonnell Douglas via API; left and right, via MEL. Page 1, via MEL; 3, via Bruce Robertson; 4-5, via MEL; 6-7, via MEL; 8-9, via MEL; 10-11, via MEL; 12, via MEL; 13, top via MEL, bottom API; 14-15, via MEL; 16, RAF Museum via TRH Pictures (TRH); 17, top via MEL, bottom Popperfoto; 18-19, top left via MEL, top right via Philip Jarrett, bottom via Bruce Robertson; 20, top via MEL, bottom via Bruce Robertson; 21, via TRH; 22-23, top left and bottom via Bruce Robertson, top right IWM via TRH; 24-25, via Bruce Robertson; 26, top via MEL, bottom via Bruce Robertson; 27, via Bruce Robertson; 28-29 via Bruce Robertson; 30-31 via Bruce Robertson; 32-32, top left and top right, via Philip Jarrett, bottom via Bruce Robertson; 34, via Bruce Robertson; 35, top and center via Bruce Robertson, bottom via MEL; 36-37, top left and right via Bruce Robertson, bottom via Philip Jarrett; 38, via MEL; 39, top via Bruce Robertson, bottom via MEL; 40-41, via Bruce Robertson; 42, top Popperfoto, bottom via Philip Jarrett; ; 43, top via MEL, bottom Popperfoto; 44-45, via MEL; 46-47; top and right, via Bruce Robertson, bottom left, via Philip Jarrett; 48-49, top via MEL, right via Bruce Robertson; 50-51, top and right via Bruce Robertson; bottom left via Philip Jarrett; 52, via Bruce Robertson; 53, top via Bruce Robertson, bottom via Philip Jarrett; 54, top via Philip Jarrett, bottom via Bruce Robertson; 55, top via MEL, bottom via Philip Jarrett; 56, bottom left, via Philip Jarrett; 57, top via MEL, bottom via Bruce Robertson; 58-58, via Bruce Robertson; 60, via Philip Jarrett; 61, top via MEL, bottom via TRH; 62-63, via TRH; 64, top via TRH, bottom via Philip Jarrett; 65, via TRH; 66-67, via MEL; 68, via MEL; 69, via Bruce Robertson; 70, top via Philip Jarrett, bottom API; 71, top via Bruce Robertson, bottom via MEL; 72-73, top and right via

MEL, bottom left via Bruce Robertson; 74, via MEL; 75, via Philip Jarrett; 76-77, via Bruce Robertson; 78, top via MEL, bottom via Bruce Robertson; 79, top via Bruce Robertson, center API, bottom via Philip Jarrett; 80-81, via Bruce Robertson; 82-83, via Philip Jarrett; 84-85, left via Bruce Robertson, top right via TRH, bottom Popperfoto; 86-87, via MEL; 88-89, top left and right via Philip Jarrett, bottom via MEL; 90-91, via MEL; 92, top via Bruce Robertson, bottom via MEL; 93, via MEL; 94, API; 95, via MEL; 96, via Bruce Robertson; 97, top via MEL, bottom via Bruce Robertson; 98-99, via MEL; 100, top via MEL, bottom via Bruce Robertson; 101, Bruce Robertson; 102-103, via Bruce Robertson; 104, top via Bruce Robertson, bottom via MEL; 105, top via Philip Jarrett, bottom via Bruce Robertson; 106-107, top and bottom right via Bruce Robertson, bottom left via MEL; 108-109, top left, USAF via TRH, bottom left via Philip Jarrett, right via MEL; 110-111, left via Bruce Robertson, right via MEL; 112, via Bruce Robertson; 113, top via Bruce Robertson, bottom via MEL; 114 via Philip Jarrett; 115, via Mike Spick; 116-117, top via MEL, bottom API; 118-119, top and bottom left, via Mike Spick, bottom right via Bruce Robertson; 120-121, top via MEL, bottom left via Bruce Robertson Popperfoto; 122-123, top left via MEL, bottom API, top right and bottom via MEL; 124, top via Philip Jarret, bototm via MEL; 125, top via MEL, bottom via Mike Spick; 126, top API, bottom via MEL; 127, via MEL; 128-129, top left/bottom right API, top right/bottom right via MEL; 130 top via MEL, bottom via Mike Spick; 131, top API, bottom via MEL; 132-133, API; 134, via TRH; 135, via Mike Spick; 136-137, top, left and bottom right, API, centre via Mike Spick; 138-139, top via Mike Spick, bottom right API; 140, top via Mike Spick, bottom API; 141, via Mike Spick.